Published in 2020 byJosiah Plumley

The author is not a licensed practitioner, physician, or medical professional and offers no medical diagnoses, treatments, suggestions, or counseling. The information presented herein has not been evaluated by the U.S. Food and Drug Administration, and it is not intended to diagnose, treat, cure, or prevent any disease. Full medical clearance from a licensed physician should be obtained before beginning or modifying any diet, exercise, or lifestyle program, and physicians should be informed of all nutritional changes.

The author claims no responsibility to any person or entity for any liability, loss, or damage caused or alleged to be caused directly or indirectly as a result of the use, application, or interpretation of the information presented herein.

Cover design by F J Moraga

ISBN-13: 978-0-578-66618

TABLE OF CONTENTS

The Most Important Questions

Stop.

No, seriously, these first three pages are the most important.

The ultimately limited resource of your time is important to me just like it should be important to you. Since your time is so valuable, I want to be sure our time together is exceptionally valuable.

So stop.

If your answer is ‘no ’to the following two questions at the bottom of this page, I sincerely want you to put the book down. Information you can’t or won’t take action on is meaningless. I’m not here to raise awareness. I am here to guide you on your journey. It’s only a journey if you are ready to move. I am writing this to help you create meaningful change in your life - to help you recognize, own, use, and ultimately grow the power you already have to make your life and health better. If you’re not ready to make a change, that’s ok. But put down this book because it’s a waste of your invaluable time. Pick it up again when you are ready.

This is a limited time offer - not because this information will go away if you don't act now, but because you have limited time and this information will only be valuable to you if you're ready to act now.

There are two things that no book, teacher, or coach, no matter how inspiring, talented, or influential can do for you - 1) Be committed for you and 2) Prevent you from procrastinating. In the following pages, you will have to face the distinction between your intentions and your actions. It will get uncomfortable as we start dismantling even valid excuses. There may be the pain of regret for not taking action earlier in life. You could get overwhelmed by all that may need to change or the fact that, if you master everything in this book in detail, you'll have only mastered the tip of the iceberg.

Actually, I take that back. You'll have mastered the bottom-most base of the iceberg - the attitude, perspective, and necessary discomfort that anchor the gleaming white showpieces at the surface.

But I can promise that, if you stick with it, you will come out on the other side with a greater sense and appreciation for the power you have, you will live and feel better, and you will have the fundamentals necessary to flesh out your own journey of discovery for your optimal health.

Ready for the questions?

1) Are you 100% committed to doing what is necessary to get healthier?

2) Are you ready to make decisions, take action, and move forward towards your goal beginning right now?

If you can't say 'yes 'to the second question, then your honest answer to the first question is 'no'. And if you can't say 'yes 'to the first question, sincerely, put this book down.

Why Am I Talking?

We get less quality sleep than ever. We deal with a greater variety of stresses than ever. We have less economic stability than ever. The winds of change seem to switch directions faster than an Olympic ping-pong match - way faster than the time it takes to find our feet. Much seems to be out of our control. We never have enough money. We never have enough time. There are a million things we are supposed to do and so many days go by watching none of them get done because we are trying to do all of them. We're exhausted, overwhelmed, and broke.

And the health stats show it.

Obesity is reaching higher levels than ever before. Type II Diabetes is on the rise. Cancer is on the rise. Prescriptions for anxiety and depression are now the rule rather than the exception. And nowhere is this epidemic more visible than the poor and middle classes.

But I don't know this because I read a bunch of stats on a website. I knew it before I ever touched a book on nutrition. It was so ingrained into my experiences growing up that I truly thought that was just how things were. I grew up poor and bore witness to all the stresses that come with it. Which important bills could be paid? Would it be possible to eat fewer times per day to save money? There was just enough money in the budget to pay for gas to get to work and back to pay for the gas to get to work and back. The stress on our family was both acute and chronic. If someone had come into our family and lectured our eating habits when we had a hard enough time even putting food on the table, they would have received a withering look of anger and frustration - well-deserved.

The situation was similar for many of the people we knew. Eating healthy was for rich people with cushy jobs and too much time on their hands. Organic kale is the last thing on your mind when you're trying to figure out how to get enough gas to get to work. The last feeling in the world you have in times like these is the feeling of *power.*

Broke is not just a lack of money. Broke is also a feeling - a feeling of having nothing to spare. It almost always refers to a lack of money. However, much more than money, it ultimately encompasses a perceived lack of *power.*

Anything that is “broke” is either not functioning at all or not functioning the way it should. Why?

Because it can’t.

There is something wrong. Something missing. Something crucial to its correct operation has been crippled. That’s why we use the term “broke.” That’s exactly how we feel.

Broke is the land of severely limited choices or no choice at all. Broke feels like and looks like powerlessness - never being or having enough. “Take what you know you can take and don’t spend too much time hoping or looking for something different because whatever you want, whatever you have will never be enough to get it.” You’re broke/n.

And that’s exactly how I felt - broke/n. When I left to launch my own life, I thought it would be different. I was intent on new beginnings. I had next to nothing but I optimistically saw that as a blank slate. Unfortunately, that slate wasn’t completely blank. I was seeing and defining my reality through a cracked and jaded screen - and I had no idea it was cracked or jaded. I just thought I was being “real.”

Gratefully, while still in my broke/n state, I accidentally stumbled upon fitness. Someone I looked up to posted on his social media about a great new podcast he was learning a lot from - Barbell Shrugged. Curious, I looked it up. That mention and the impulse to check it out led me down a long, winding, rocky, and beautiful road to the person I am today, the industry I am in, and the way I serve others.

In short, the hosts and guests on Barbell Shrugged introduced me to the science of fitness in a way I had never encountered it. Up to that point, I thought being fit was all about calisthenics, running, and beating yourself to a pulp.

They introduced me to the variable goals and tools of relative strength, absolute strength, mobility, technique, speed, power, anaerobic capacity, etc.

In other words, it wasn't about having an excess of time or money, being obsessive about looks or being a jock (as a self-described nerd, I was allergic to the term). It was about defining what you want to be capable of doing and choosing the path of mastery to achieve it. It was about applying scientific principles, curiosity, and a disciplined approach. It was about using the tools you had access to - whether it was just your body and the floor or a fully equipped gym - to forge yourself. That was different and that was something I could get on board with.

It was about the freedom that comes from not being limited in general by your own body. It was about the power of forging ahead, progressing, and succeeding - no permission needed. No one else's will, mood, whim, or fancy could hold me back. What I put in was what I would get out. Period. In a time when I felt powerless to effect most things in my life, finding a point where I actually had control was crucial and life changing. It became the first domino.

Unlike dominoes, however, unleashing the rest wasn't easy or quick.

I had a lot to learn and unlearn. Learning was the easy part. I've excelled at learning my entire life. I dove into it with confidence and intensity. I admit, however, that there was, and is still, a lot more to learn than I ever imagined. It was the unlearning, however, which delayed me the most. To unlearn something, you must first realize that there is something to unlearn. It is difficult to question your own assumptions when you are certain they are reality.

For example, I had always believed gyms were too expensive for me. It never occurred to me that they might be affordable. Fortunately, you can only listen to so many podcasts mentioning dead lifting techniques before you simply must go find a barbell. This lead me to enter a gym for the first time. Huh! Turns out that cutting back on a few fast food meals was all it took for me to afford it. Who knew!? "Gyms are too expensive" was one of the first assumptions I unlearned and it would certainly not be the last.

The next big hurdle was nutrition. I had always assumed I needed to make a lot more money in order to afford healthy meals. A quick side-by-side look at the cost of organic kale and the Fast Food Dollar Menu was usually enough to convince me I was correct. As I started to learn more about nutrition and pay attention to what I was consuming, my assumptions began to break down. I would catch myself being up-sold at the drive thru to a full meal that cost me $7- $10. I then passed packets of tuna in the grocery store and noticed they were less than $1! Sure, they weren't organic, but they were certainly better than junk food by any measure and, surprisingly, a lot cheaper.

Little by little, my assumption that eating healthy was too expensive fell apart. As I experimented to find cheaper and faster ways to eat healthy, practicing what I now preach, my former assumption began to look incredibly ridiculous and obviously incorrect. Same person, different lenses - one was based on unquestioned assumptions while the other was based in science, experimentation, and years of practice.

In the process of learning, I am still unlearning things. Having unlearned so many things, I am much more proactive about questioning my own beliefs and keeping an open and curious mind. It is a process - often a long one. It seems almost embarrassing to me now, but just the few examples I gave above took me a couple years to fully realize AFTER I started delving into fitness. I can be pretty stubborn.

In the process of learning and unlearning, I went from being broke, weak, and unhealthy to broke, weak, and healthy, to broke, strong, and healthy to doing much better financially, strong, and healthy. Step by step, I was able to recognize and take hold of the few things - nutrition and fitness - which were reliably in my control. This practice gave me permission to recognize and take hold of more aspects of my life that I once thought were outside of my reach - my relationships, the way I worked, the way I planned, etc. It didn't happen all at once. In many ways, it is still happening. As I write this, I have never been stronger, healthier, or more free. I have accomplished more than I ever dreamed, helped more people in a shorter amount of time than I ever thought possible, and can't help but smile as I see how far I've come and look to how far I dare to go.

That's the point. You can too. You can begin by taking the little scraps that others call nothing and leveraging them into something. You can take that something and turn it into something more. You can take that something more and turn it into the life you want to live.

But that journey doesn't start by waiting until 'something more' pops in your lap. You start with the scraps that others call nothing.

Know What You Want

You picked up this book for a reason. What is that reason?

Is it to get healthier? Do you want to lose weight? Are you hoping for more energy? In all honesty, you can have a million reasons for picking up this book, and as long as they are stuck in the hazy, blurry, and unfocused land of wishful thinking, not a single one of them will matter. The best reason and the worst reason have the same outcome if no action is taken.

To get to any goal, not just with nutrition, you must be crystal clear about what EXACTLY you want to achieve and then break it down into daily tasks. It DOES NOT matter if the goal is the perfect goal. You can absolutely define an exact goal and be committed to it while also being open to the possibility that that goal might change as you learn and grow. It only matters that it is achievable in a measurable way AND that you know exactly what those measurements should be. If you're having a hard time doing this, simply start with your general goal and ask one question over and over until you narrow it down to a specific and measurable goal. That question is," How will I know I've achieved my goal?" The point is to find out what you specifically want and then break it down to a general timeline. After that, you need to break it down into actions small enough to take action on today.

Example:

I want to be healthier! —> How will I know I've achieved that? —> When I lose weight. —> How much weight? —> Between 20 and 30 pounds. —> 20 or 30? —> Let's go with 30 pounds.

Once you have decided on your goal, you need to identify the timeline within which you want to accomplish this goal.

Example:

How soon do I want to lose the 30 pounds? —> Tomorrow! —> .... Ok, let's go for 30 weeks.

Once you have decided on your measurable goal and have a specific timeline you want to accomplish it in, the next step is to break both the goal and the timeline down into the smallest reasonable sections so you can start planning week to week and even day to day. If you can't break a year long plan into small enough pieces that you can take action on today, that year long plan is worth nothing.

Example:

I am losing 30 pounds in 30 weeks. —> That means I need to lose an average of 4-5 pounds every month. —> To do that, I need to lose an average of 1 pound per week.

What you've just done is break down the big thing that seems way out of reach into the next little thing that is well within your grasp RIGHT NOW! Losing 30 pounds may seem like a lot, but losing 1 pound this week is very doable. In fact, if you break down the math, you can easily take action today by eating exactly what you need to maintain and burning 500 extra calories, eating 500 calories less than you need to maintain your weight and not exercising at all, or any combination of both.

Once again, the point isn't to have a perfect goal. The point is to have a clear goal you can take action on today. You will learn to set better goals only through the experience that comes through taking action. You won't take action if you're frozen by trying to figure out the "perfect goal" or the "perfect plan."

Identifying What You Have

Everyone in the world has their own biases and assumptions. No one lives a purely assumption-free life. One of the most damaging assumptions broke people tend to have is "I can't..." This assumption is completely understandable. We often spent our entire childhoods being told that we couldn't. We couldn't go to the concert all our friends were going to because we couldn't afford the entry fee. We couldn't go anywhere because we couldn't afford the extra gas. We couldn't get the new shoes because we could barely afford the $20 shoes we got eight months ago. While we were likely being told the absolute truth, a reactive mindset was being formed. We often assume "I can't" without questioning if it is actually true.

To grow out of this mindset, you must learn to question your assumptions. This book is going to annihilate two common assumptions about health - 1) Eating healthy is too expensive and 2) Meal prepping takes too much time.

The insidious nature of powerlessness is that it is self reinforcing. It teaches you to remain powerless, even when you are not. Psychologists call this learned helplessness. The more you believe that things are outside of your control, the less you will try. When you grow up poor, it is easy to learn that you are helpless. See a car you like? You can't get it. See a gym you want to join? You can't afford it. Want to take a vacation? With what time off and with what money? When you are constantly faced with things you want that are always out of reach, it is easy to be convinced that they will always be out of reach. You are powerless. At least, that's what you've been led to believe.

It's also what you've chosen to believe.

While you focus in on all the evidence of your lack of power piling up in the form of things you cannot do, the bank accounts of billionaires are being filled by the little things you can do. Some of the biggest and most profitable companies in the world are built on the very things you feel you don't have. Think you have no money? The largest retail store in the world makes over 10 billion dollars a year, mostly from the low-income households it is designed to target. Think you have no time? Fast food restaurants make billions of dollars a year on that assumption. It's interesting that I've never heard of someone getting through a drive-thru faster than the time it takes to heat up a lunch from home.

It may not seem like you have much power in the big things, but in the little things - you have a lot more power than you think. As any successful person will tell you - the little things are the foundation of the big things.

F.E.A.S.T.

Even a million dollars in your pocket is useless if you don't know it's there. One of the biggest assumptions that needs to be questioned is the idea that you can't afford something - that eating healthy is out of your financial reach. While we will break down just how affordable a healthy way of eating can be in coming sections, we are going to start with a little exercise that effectively reveals how much power has been slipping through our fingers in the form of cents and dollars spent on things directly harmful to us. It's called F.E.A.S.T.

Fast Food (drive-thrus or pick-ups)

Entertainment Calories (movie snacks, restaurants, sports event snacks)

Alcohol

Sugary Drinks (energy drinks, sugary coffees and teas, juices, sodas)

Tobacco (this extends to smoking or vaping anything you know to be harmful to your health)

These items aren't just non necessities. They are

directly harmful to you. Since you care about your health, they are fair game for critique. We are going to use this acronym to help uncover your individual power which you may have previously overlooked. There are individual examples you can fill in if you don't understand the examples right away.

FEAST Step 1:

Go through each category and estimate the number of times you indulge in these items per week.

FEAST Step 2:

Go through each category and estimate the low average of what you spend EACH TIME you indulge in these items.

FEAST Step 3:

Multiply the two numbers (number of times per week x cost per time) in each category together to get the average amount you spend on them per week.

FEAST Step 4:

Add all the numbers together and multiply by 4 to get the average minimum you spend as a whole each month.

If these steps seem confusing at first, plug your personal numbers into the follow example.

Example:

FEAST Step 1: Average Number Of Times Per Week

Fast Food: 2x/week Entertainment Calories: 1x/week - Restaurant or Movie Snacks Alcohol: 1x/week - 4 drinks Sugary Drinks: 5x/week - Starbucks Coffee

Tobacco: Never

FEAST Step 2: Average Dollar Amount Per Time

Fast Food: $8/order Entertainment Calories: $12/order Alcohol: $3/beer

Sugary Drinks: $5/order Tobacco: $0

FEAST Step 3: Average Amount Spend On Each Category Weekly (Step 1 x Step 2 for each category)

Fast Food: $16/week Entertainment Calories: $12/week Alcohol: $12/week Sugary Drinks: $25/week Tobacco: $0/week

FEAST Step 4: Add It All Up and Multiply By 4

Fast Food ($16) + Entertainment Calories ($12) + Alcohol ($12) + Sugary Drinks ($25) + Tobacco ($0) = $65/week

$65/week x 4 weeks = $260/month AT LEAST

What's crazy is that the preceding example is absolutely a typical one. Notice that none of the harmful categories were extreme. This is not a person who eats out every meal, drinks heavily, or even smokes. They don't even spend the normal amount when they do go out. Yet, they are still spending a car payment on hurting themselves per month!

If you knew that a friend of yours was spending almost $300/month on hurting themselves, you would be worried and try your best to talk sense into them. Often, when it comes to ourselves, however, we are blind. We accept excuses of convenience and lie to ourselves about its cost. Fast food is directly linked to cancer and diabetes. Alcohol caps off today by stealing joy from tomorrow. Sugary drinks provide a brief pick me and then pile-drive you into the ground in a mental fog a few hours later. Tobacco products steal us from our loved ones. Entertainment food contains more chemicals than a science lab. Restaurants can be good, but usually aren't. If they are...$15 for a salad made from $2 of ingredients is kind of a slap to the face. We use these things as a means of escape - a way to forget. All the while they are trapping us into the very bodies and lives we are trying to escape from. It's a sick cycle which has destroyed thousands of lives. There is a way out.

On the flip side of this tragedy is something beautiful. If you are spending money on things that hurt you, that means YOU are spending money on things that hurt you. YOU are in control. You can't control your genetics. You can't control how you grew up. You CAN control what you CHOOSE to do. Use F.E.A.S.T. as a way to put it right in front of your face. It's crazy how the world of "broke" convinces us we have no choice - how it seeks to toss what little power we have away to the most convenient or entertaining bidder. It only has this power as long as it can convince us that we don't have any ourselves. The moment you open your eyes to the power you already have, you have started your journey towards the freedom so many of us never thought we could have.

.

Identify Exactly What You Need

Once you understand what power you do have, the next step is to get strategic with it. The more limited your resources, the more strategic you should be in deploying them. Just as you need to be very specific about what you want to achieve, you must also be specific on what you need to get there. This is where we get into the discussion on macros and calories.

In case you are unfamiliar, 'Macros' is short for macronutrients. These are the nutrients we need in relatively large doses for energy, repair, and maintenance. They are Protein, Carbohydrates (Carbs), and Fats. While each of these nutrients are critical for a wide variety of processes in your body, for the purposes of this book and your goals, we are going to keep it simple.

Protein is for muscle maintenance, repair, and building.

Whole food sources of protein are *chicken, beef, turkey, fish, dairy, and specific vegetable combinations.*

Carbs are for power energy - specifically for intense activities like sprints, lifting weights, or helping someone move furniture.

Whole food sources of carbs are *rice, potatoes, oats, fruits, and vegetables.*

Fats are for endurance energy - specifically for longer lasting endurance activities such as walks, long-distance walks, and general living.

Whole food sources of fats are *meat, dairy, avocado, nuts, olive oil, coconut oil, and avocado oil.*

Remember, being broke allows you to be extra strategic. When it comes to your nutrition, everything you put in your mouth must have a purpose. Everything must help you get to where you want to go, the person you want to be, and the body you want to have. The time for handing over our power to those things which hurt us is over.

Depending on your specific goal, activity type and level, body type, and genetics, there are specific macronutrient sources, amounts, and ratios that will optimally fuel you towards attaining your goals. What many nutrition coaches do not want you to know is that it is nearly impossible to know exactly what those sources, amounts, and ratios should be for you on the very first try. Based on education and experience, we can make really good guesses as to where you should start and quickly figure out next steps, but there is no secret formula. THAT'S OK! It's meant to be a starting point from which we can base our experiments and tweaks until we do reach what is perfect for you. Reaching your goals, like everything else in life, is an iterative process - meaning that you make adjustments, some large, some small, as you go. This is VERY important. ***The 'secret' is in the messy process, not the perfect starting line.***

The starting line IS still important because it is the initial moment of ACTION. To understand your starting line, you must clearly define where you want to be and put a number on it - pounds of fat lost, pounds of muscle gained, a certain weight you want to lift, etc. You then must find out where you are right now and put a number on that too. The most helpful numbers are

Body Fat Percentage,

Scale Weight, and

Basal Metabolic Rate.

These numbers combined give us a really good idea of how much fat you actually need to lose and/or how much muscle/lean weight you have to begin with. They also allow us to come up with a starting point to estimate how many calories to plan for in a given week.

Important Note: There *is a fairly common condition called body dysmorphia. This is a mental state wherein you are unable to see your body accurately and have severe mental stress over perceived flaws. This condition, if left unchecked, can make people who are so low in body fat that they are in danger of dying still look in the mirror and believe themselves to be fat. While this is a severe case, it does have many less severe forms that can still lead to a very unhealthy view of your body and perpetual dissatisfaction regardless of what you see in the mirror. This is a disease of perception and thus makes it impossible to gauge or measure progress based on visual markers. If this is you or even might be you,* ***stick to purely objective data like tape measurements or handheld devices****. They tend to be more accurate and provide helpful information if/when you feel down about your perceived lack of progress. A tape measure will not stretch itself to match your emotions in the* *moment and a handheld body fat measurer doesn't care if you feel like you haven't progressed. And when you see the 3% body fat loss on paper, it will slowly but surely help you align your feelings with facts. Don't feel bad if this is a problem for you. I have also struggled with my feelings about how I look not matching how I actually look. Perception can be very tricky. Objective data, however, always brings me back to center.*

There are several ways to calculate Body Fat Percentage and I don't want you to get caught up in the weeds of what method is the most accurate. Especially in the beginning, our objective is progress, not perfection. That being the case, it is more important that the method you choose be consistent and the time you measure be consistent. Even if a method is 1-3% off, using the same method every time will still give you a good idea of how much progress you have made. If you're going to use tape measurements, use tape measurements for at least 12 weeks. If you're going to use a handheld calculator, same thing. If you're going to use a visual test, keep using a visual test. Understanding your Body Fat Percentage and your weight will give you a good idea of how much actual fat you have and how much fat you really need to lose. For many, the amount of fat they really need to lose to get to the body they feel great in is significantly less than they imagine. The point is to get the data so you can begin tracking. I have included two links to websites which provide quick, convenient, and free calculators.

To test based on tape measurements tape measurements (https://www.calculator.net/body-fat-calculator.html)

To test based on the mirror (https://www.ruled.me/visually-estimate-

body-fat-percentage/)

Once you have the percentage, multiply it by your scale weight to get your total fat pounds. DON'T WORRY! That is NOT how much you need to lose. Use one of the measure estimate resources above and fill in the blanks below.

Body Fat Percentage x Scale Weight = Total Pounds Of Fat

_____________ x ____________=

____

First, decide what percentage of body fat you want to achieve. If your goal is general health, depending on age, most women are optimally healthy between 20-30% with 15% being a general lower limit for a non-competition 'walking around' percentage. Most men are optimally healthy between 15-20% with 8-10% being a general lower limit for a non-competition 'walking around' percentage. Once you decide, what percentage you want to reach, go get a standard calculator and perform the following calculations. There will be pages right afterwards on which you can place your personal numbers.

Example. Let's say you are 250 pounds and estimate your Body Fat Percentage to be 25% and you want it to be 12%. Then the calculations would go as follows:

1. Scale Weight x Body Fat Percentage = Pounds of Total Fat

250 x .25 = 62.5

2. Scale Weight - Pounds of Total Fat = Lean Weight

250 - 62.5 = 187.5

3. Lean Weight / (1 - Percent Body Fat Goal) = Goal Weight

187.5 / (1 - 12) —> 187.5 / .88 = 213 (round to nearest whole number)

4. Scale Weight - Goal Weight = Goal for Pounds of Fat Lost

250 - 213 =-------------------- > 37 < --------

Remember, for steps 1and 3 that the you use decimals in calculations that speak of percentages. Therefore, if you are 30% Body Fat, you don't write [Scale Weight x 301. You write [Scale Weight x .31. Likewise, if you want to be 15% body fat, you don't write (1 - 15). You write (1 - .15). Math matters.

1. Scale Weight x Body Fat Percentage = Pounds of Total Fat

______________ x _____________=

____

2. Scale Weight - Pounds of Total Fat = Lean Weight

_____________ -_______________

____

3. Lean Weight / (1 - Percent Body Fat Goal) = Goal Weight

__________ / (1 - ________) =

____

4. Scale Weight - Goal Weight = Goal for Pounds of Fat Lost

______________ - __________= -------->

______________<-----------

As a general guideline to decide, I want to make two distinct points. Firstly, remember, we are choosing your END goal as you want it right now. We will, of course, break that goal into smaller, bite- size goals to help prevent overwhelm. You don’t need to get it perfectly right at this very moment. You have all the permission in the world to adjust your goals as you develop in understanding your own body. The imperfect goal you can take action on immediately is infinitely better than avoiding action because you want to figure out the “perfect goal.” Most of the information you need to set your “perfect” goal can only be found on the road to the imperfect one.

Secondly, avoid setting your goals based on being “realistic” instead of what you actually want. I have spoken with thousands of individuals to help them set their goals. Almost every time I hear, “I want to be realistic,” what they are really saying is,” I don’t think I can do it,” or ,” I have been unhealthy for so long that I can’t imagine successfully reaching and maintaining a healthy body" - in other words selling themselves short of what they actually want and what they are actually capable of accomplishing. If this is something you struggle with, I encourage you to give yourself permission to go after what you really want. I know it can be scary - fear of disappointing yourself and/or others or even thinking you aren't worth achieving your goals are very common struggles when embarking on a journey of health. However, I am wildly confident that if you follow the process, learn and cultivate curiosity about your body and health, and refuse to quit, you can achieve goals beyond what you will allow yourself to imagine even now and will find joy in the process. I'm not just saying this to say it. I've seen it happen hundreds of times. I make this statement based on observational data.

The other important measurement to look at is your Basal Metabolic Rate - or BMR. This is important because it gives an educated starting guess as to how many calories you burn every day. You can do this a few different ways and I encourage you to look into it (because science is fun!). However, for the sake of simplicity, I have included a link below to a site that will allow you to enter some basic information, add your activity level, and come up with a helpful estimate of how many calories you are burning in a given day.

Estimate Your Caloric Needs (https://www.calculator.net/bmr-calculator.html)

Make sure to record that number for later use.

Once you have a workable estimate of how many calories you are burning every day, you must then return to your goals. If your goal is fat loss, a completely reasonable rate of loss is 1-2 pounds of fat per week ON AVERAGE. Some weeks will be more. Some weeks may be less. Over the course of 1-2 months, you can definitely lose 1-2 pounds of fat per week on average. Let's assume you want to be on the more aggressive side and push to lose 2 pounds of fat per week. To do that, you need to burn around 1,000 more calories than you consume.

For the sake of easy math, let's assume you naturally burn around 2,500 calories per day on average. To lose 2 pounds of fat per week, you can eat 500 calories less than average (2,000) AND burn 500 calories more than average (3,000) every day. This will lead to a total of a 1,000 calorie deficit. You can also maintain your normal activity level and, instead, choose to eat 1,000 calories less than average (1,500) every day.

If you can set aside a total of an hour a day for a fast-paced walk, you may want to choose moderate exercise AND caloric restriction. It doesn't necessarily have to be a continuous hour of fast-paced walking. If you can get in two 30-minute walks per day or three 20- minute walks per day after meals, you will get a similar effect. If you can't, you may want to opt for simple caloric restriction.

Now that you have decided how many calories you need to eat per day to hit your goal, we can introduce macronutrient ratios. First, let's have a quick discussion about the kind of food we need to be eating. Foremost, we want everything we eat and drink to have a purpose beyond just taste. One of the goals we should always be striving for is overall health. A person who looks great but is constantly tired or sick can't really enjoy the body they have forged. If you're going after a goal, you must be very specific about the terms you are using. The first term we must clarify, and the one with the most fireworks attached to it, is the word 'healthy.'

There are libraries of books arguing for one diet over another - everything from eating only raw meat to eating only raw vegetables. It gets overwhelming very quickly if you try to find the "best" diet. However, when you're broke, it makes no sense to spend all your time and money to find a magical "best" diet while you're still eating fast food, drinking Kool-Aid, and downing sugary snacks.

For the purposes of this book, we're going to keep it very simple. ***If you could hunt, harvest, and make it in Nature, it's fair game. If it needed to go through a few factories and get mixed with a bunch of extra chemicals before it got to you, avoid it like the poison it generally is.***

How does this play out in real life? Could you go harvest rice in nature? Absolutely! Could you go in the woods and find sugary cereal? Probably not. Could you go get a steak in nature? It is absolutely possible. Could you get a campfire together and create lunch "meat"? Not a chance. While this isn't a perfect rule, it successfully rules out 95% of nonsense "food" that does nothing good for your body. A long-term, healthy way of eating is almost exclusively made up of real, whole foods - avoiding harmfully processed foods as much as possible.

Given the above paragraph, we are going to

make the assumption from this point forward that the food we are strategizing with will be 'real' food - as close to God's green earth as possible before it hits your mouth. That being said, we will now reveal the magic formula.

The Magic Formula

Calculating Your Macros

40/30/30

That's it! That is all you really need to get started. Is it perfect? No. Does it work for most people? Yes. Is the real intention that you use it as a starting point and then experiment every 8 weeks to see what YOUR body best responds to? Absolutely!

What does 40/30/30 stand for?

40% of your calories come from protein. 30% of your calories come from carbohydrates.

30% of your calories come from fat.

Referring to the above examples, let's say that you naturally burn 2,500 calories on a daily basis. Let's also assume that you are willing to contribute an extra hour every day to a vigorous walk (or really anything that keeps your heart rate elevated). If this is the case, then you will need to eat approximately

2.0 calories per day in order to be at a

1.0 calorie daily deficit and thus lose 2 pounds of

fat per week on average. That means that you will need:

200 grams of protein/day (2,000 calories x .4 = 800 calories; 800 calories / 4 calories per gram of protein = 200 grams of protein per day)

150 grams of carbs/day (2,000 calories x .3 = 600 calories; 600 calories / 4 calories per gram of carbs = 150 grams of carbs per day)

67 grams of fat/day

(2,000 calories x .3 = 600 calories; 600 calories / 9 calories per grams of fat = 67 grams of fat per day)

Each gram of protein is 4 calories.

Each gram of carbs is 4 calories.

Each gram of fat is 9 calories.

Once you know your average caloric burn per day and whether you want to lose 1 pound or 2 pounds of fat per week, you can calculate the calories you need to plan for on a daily basis.

Just plug your own daily individual caloric need you

got from the link to reach your goals in to the formulas below. If you missed the link, you can find it again here.

Protein

1. Daily Calories Needed For Goals x .4
= **Daily Calories Needed from Protein**

(For Fat Loss, Calories Needed for 2 pounds of fat loss per week are Your Maintenance Calories - 500 if you are working out OR Your Maintenance Calories - 1,000 if you are not working out.)

_________________________ x .4 =

—> __________________________ <—

2. **Daily Calories Needed from Protein**

(seen above)/ 4 = Daily Grams of Needed Protein

_________________________ / 4 =

—> __________________________ <—

Carbs

1. Daily Calories Needed For Goals x .3

= Daily Calories Needed from Carbs

______________________________x .3 =

—>______________________________ <—

2. **Daily Calories Needed from Carbs**

(seen above)/ 4 = Daily Grams of Needed Carbs

______________________________/ 4 =

—>______________________________<—

Fat

1. Daily Calories Needed For Goals x .3
= Daily Calories Needed from Fat

______________________________x .3 =

—>______________________________<—

2. Daily Calories Needed from Fat

(seen above) / 9 = Daily Grams of Needed Fat

______________________________/ 9 =

—>______________________________ <—

You will use those final three numbers to plan your meals for the day and, ultimately, the plan for the week.

Refocus, Save Time, Save Money

I realize that, for many people, all this math work is starting to make meal planning drier than a saltine cracker covered in cinnamon (if you don't know what I mean...try it). To counter this, I am going to take a moment and refocus on why you are doing this to begin with.

Why are we calculating macros? Why are we taking the time to figure out Body Fat Percentage and BMR and Macro Ratios? Isn't this all a bit much? If you are finding yourself asking this question, I fully understand where you are coming from. If you consider yourself in the category of "broke" and "busy," this may seem like just a bunch of extra work. While I do understand why it may appear that way, let me explain why it is actually the opposite.

The way most people go through life is reactive - draining you dry from the sheer number of daily on-the-spot decisions they make. They spend time and energy in the morning deciding what to have for breakfast, making it, and often feeling slightly bad about their decision. They do the same for lunch - often choosing a convenient fast food option. They then do the exact same thing for dinner.

Think about it. The average person reacts to their hunger, spends mental energy deciding what to eat, physical (and often financial) energy getting the food, and emotional energy regretting it THREE TIMES A DAY - and that's assuming they don't want snacks! That equates to at least 90 energy drains a month with nothing to show for it but declining health.

By doing the hard work up front, we are bringing 90 scattered energy expenditures down to 4 focused energy expenditures. Instead of spending mental energy 3 times a day to decide what to eat, you decide in a single session 1 time a week. Instead of spending physical energy and time to get the food 2-3 times a day, you bring it down to 2 hours on 1 day a week and 1 minute every morning. Instead of spending an average of $50- $150 a week on junk food, fast food, and restaurants ON TOP OF groceries, you are bringing it down to $40-$70 a week for an entire week of healthy food. Instead of adding daily stress to your life due to your food choices, you are making a healthy decision by planning the whole week of healthy food and having no need to stress about choices. They have already been decided, prepared, and are ready to go.

To simplify this, you are saving up to 20 mini-planning sessions, a minimum of 8 hours, up to $440, and an immeasurable amount of psychological stress IN JUST ONE WEEK!

That's 80 decisions you don't have to make, 32 hours you don't have to spend, $200-$1,000 you don't have to waste, and a palpable weight off of your mind IN EVERY MONTH!

That's 1,040 decisions you don't have to make, 1,664 hours (well over two months) you don't have to spend, $2,400-$12,000 you no longer waste, and a much healthier mind IN ONE YEAR!

Yes, I am very confident in stating that this will make your life easier, simpler, and much less expensive. A little planning on the front-end of your nutrition for the week can really save you that much. Doing the math is worth it.

The Power Of Being Scrappy

The second reason is about power. As you have already read, feeling broke is about feeling powerless. There is so much you want to do but don't think you have the money to do. There is so much you want to provide for yourself and your family but your bank account seems to exist just to laugh away your dreams. This can be especially true when it comes to being fit and healthy. You tell yourself you want to start eating right, but then you look at the cost of health food and you're unsure how you would make it. You tell yourself you want to be fit, but a gym seems too expensive, equipment seems too expensive, and maybe the area you live in isn't exactly the greatest for running or walking around. You have the desire. You have the will. You don't see the path. How do you stretch when it seems you're already hanging on by a thread?

The power inherent in being broke is that we are used to being scrappy just to survive. That resilience, hardness, and creativity combined with structure, strategy, and a dash of hope give you a serious edge against a task/journey that would crush those who haven't had to do go through anything difficult. Life has slapped you down and you have gotten back up countless times, or else you wouldn't be reading this. Even though you feel weak, helpless, or powerless, the dozens, hundreds, or even thousands of times getting back up again matter. Those. Reps. Matter. They are a showcase of strength - even if you don't feel it. That strength just needs a fighting chance to channel you into more than getting back up over and over again.

There are loads of experts out there who talk about the big decisions that can make a big difference - which 401k to use, how to invest, buy or rent, and, my personal favorite, what obscure supplement from the distant Mountains of Foolery that costs half your income but gives you a slight edge in your journey. None of those things really matter because 1) you can't take action on them now and 2) you're too preoccupied just trying to stay standing.

If you wait until you feel you can make big moves, you may be waiting forever. If you begin to master the tiny decisions, the slight edges, the inch-long steps forward, you gain a power that no one can take away from you. Pull your power from the pennies in your hand instead of the dollars in your dreams. Movement breeds momentum. Momentum multiplies movement. Let it be very clear - movement comes first.

Finishing Your Macro Calculations

Alright, now that we have taken a math break, it's time to get back to it. Let's return to the four numbers we have come to:

1. Number of calories you need to eat to lose about 2 pounds per week

2. Grams of Protein needed per day =

3. Grams of Carbs needed per day =

4. Grams of Fat needed per day =

If you have forgotten what your numbers are, go back to the previous pages and fill in the blanks, do the math, and you'll have them ready.

We are going to continue to use the example of a person who has a daily metabolic burn of 2,500 calories. Their strategy to lose 2 pounds of fat per week is to burn an extra 500 calories per day (making their daily metabolic burn 3,000 calories) and eating 500 calories less (making their daily caloric consumption 2,000 calories).

Pro Tip: If you have a significant amount of excess fat to lose, this aggressive approach is completely appropriate. However, as you get close to your goal, readjust your planned calories to 500 calorie deficit instead of 1,000. If you go aggressive all the way until you reach your goal and then decide to, all of a sudden, return to no deficit at all, you will likely gain some fat back since you have trained your body and metabolism to operate at a lower rate. Raising up your calories more gradually as you get close to your goal may make your journey a little longer, but you will be more easily able to sustain the finish line once you reach it. There is no point in rushing to a finish line if the way you do so will keep you from staying there.

As a reminder, this person will be starting with a template of 40% Protein, 30% Carbs, and 30% Fat. That means their numbers will be 200 grams of Protein per day, 150 grams of Carbs per day, and 67 grams of Fat per day.

We must now strategize on how many times we are able to consistently eat per day. Remember, the consistent average is far more important than a perfect day. Some research says that eating small meals 6 times per day is best for fat loss. Others say that eating 1 time per day (intermittent fasting) is best.

Either way will work if you are eating at a caloric deficit and there are pros and cons to both sides. However, it is far more important to look at your own life, schedule, and family practices.

If you can only consistently commit to 3 meals per day, then that is exactly what we will strategize around. 80% perfect consistently applied is infinitely better than 100% perfect that isn't applied. For the purposes of this exercise, let's assume this person can only realistically commit to 3 meals per day. That means that we need to take at least the Grams of Protein for the day and divide them by 3 to get what we need per meal.

Pro Tip*: This is one area where a high quality protein supplement CAN be helpful. If the goal is fat loss, I recommend getting a Whey Isolate - bonus points if it's hydrolyzed. This can be used around your walk or other workout and allows you to lower your protein needs in the other meals. The typical container is 30 servings and contains 25-30 grams of protein per serving. You can use it as a protein-only '4th meal.' Now, why am I saying that a supplement CAN help when the point of this book is to lower costs and save money? Because the price of this '4th meal' will run you anywhere from $1- $1.50 per day. That's cheaper* *than the value menu at a drive-thru. The only difference is that you will be paying for the whole month up front. This often makes it seem more expensive than it actually is if you break it down to a daily amount. If you can do so, great! Simply subtract the grams of protein in the scoop from your daily protein need and divide the rest by 3. If you can't, don't worry about it. It is a helpful option, NOT a need. 200 grams of protein per day divided by 3 meals per day is around 67 grams of protein. While eating that much protein in one sitting is not the MOST ideal for efficient protein absorption and muscle synthesis, it will still get you to where you want to go.*

Finding Your Serving Size and Planning Your Meals

This is where we get into the art of "serving size." Serving size, like some other health recommendations, is based on an aggregated national average. While looking at serving sizes on food products is a helpful tool to know exactly what you're getting, that doesn't mean you should read it as YOUR serving size. Every month, if you adjust your number of meals, macro ratios, or number of total calories needed, some quick math recalibration will hone in your serving size again. Your personal serving size will change as your goals change and as you get better and better at discovering what works best for your body.

Remember that we are using real, whole foods only. This actually makes this a lot easier because these types of food tend to be more standard in their macro measurements based on weight and volume. What this also means is that you have to calculate the macros based on ALL of the raw ingredients. If you're only working with chicken breast, then you can calculate very easily. However, you can't consider 4 oz of chicken salad to have the same macros as 4 oz of chicken breast. It simply doesn't. You can make a homemade chicken salad if you count the macros you're putting in from the other ingredients as part of your carbs and fat. You can't count a store- bought chicken salad AS chicken breast. Oatmeal cookies don't count as oatmeal (neither do flavored oatmeal packets). Chips don't count as potatoes (neither do fries). You get the point.

Back to the task at hand - calculating YOUR serving size. If this person needs 200 grams of protein and is eating 3 times per day, they need around 67 grams of protein per meal - meaning 67 grams of protein is their serving size. I am including some of the most common forms of lean protein in 1 ounce increments. This will make the math easier in the long run.

Chicken Breast 9g/oz Ground Turkey 8g/oz Top Sirloin Steak 8g/oz Ground Beef (85% Lean) 5g/oz 1 Whole Egg 6g/egg 1 Cup of Egg Whites 26g/cup

The next step is to decide which sources of protein you want to use for the coming week. There is no right answer for this so you have to find what works for you. As a starting point, I personally recommend choosing 2-4 different protein sources for the week. In my experience, choosing 1 leads quickly to boredom and temptation to eat off-plan. Choosing more than 4 often frustrates the meal prep process so that it is too complicated or time consuming and the temptation is heightened to simply not do it. I find that having 1-2 standard proteins for breakfast (eggs and ground turkey in my case) and 2 other proteins to choose from for the rest of the day is the sweet spot of both variety and simplicity - both important factors in sticking to a particular way of eating.

Let's err on the side of more complicated in the example so you can see how easy it really can be. For the next week, we are choosing 4 different protein sources. This person wants to eat eggs and ground turkey for breakfast and have a choice between top sirloin steak and chicken breast for lunch and dinner. To be clear, we are planning for 7 breakfasts, 7 lunches, and 7 dinners since they can only eat 3 times per day for 7 days a week.

Pro Tip: *When we are figuring out the exact amounts needed per meal, we will often find odd numbers such as 7.7 ounces or 4.3 grams. While some of you may find it fun to be as precise as possible, nutritionally, being off by a tenth of an ounce (or even half an ounce) isn't going to make or break you. Easy math that gets you close and that you are willing to do consistently will* *always win over someone who gets overwhelmed trying to be perfect. That being said, when we calculate for how many ounces of a particular protein is needed, a good rule of thumb is to round DOWN to the nearest whole number if you're trying to lose fat and round UP to the nearest whole number if you are trying to gain muscle. This means that, if you are trying to lose weight, if you find you need 4.2 ounces of ground turkey per meal, round DOWN to 4 ounces. This will make it much easier to plan AND measure.*

Pro Tip**: Some people have grocery stores which will cut the exact amount they want for every meat. Many people do not. For those of us who don't, this is for you.* ***Find your total number of ounces needed for the week for each protein. *Once that is completed, round the resulting amount to the nearest pound (16 ounces each). Say, for example, that you find you need 49 ounces of Top Sirloin, but your grocery store only sells them by the pound. The closest pound is 3 pounds (48 ounces). Your grocery plan will therefore say 3 pounds of Top Sirloin.*

***Pro Tip**: When calculating protein measurements for meat, it is always assumed to be raw. If you have a scale, measure your food BEFORE you cook it to make certain the right amount of protein is in each* *serving. If you measure cooked meat, it will be inaccurate as cooking completely changes the weight depending on how and how long you cook it but it doesn't change the protein content at all.*

Breakfast

Breakfast consists of eggs and ground turkey. Presumably, this means we want half of the protein to come from eggs and half of the protein to come from the ground turkey. Since we need 67 grams of protein for breakfast, we simply divide it by 2 in order to get how many grams of protein is needed from each one. In this case, 67 divided by 2 is 33.5 grams of protein each.

Now, take the chart for Whole Eggs and divide 33.5 by the 6 grams of protein in each egg. This comes out to 5.6 eggs.

I will say this repeatedly, the consistent average that is close enough is better than a perfect day you can't repeat. Clearly, you can't make 5.6 eggs. So, since the goal is fat loss, round down to 5 eggs.

Secondly, take the chart for Ground Turkey and divide 33.5 by the 8 grams of protein in each ounce. This comes out to 4.2 ounces. As suggested above, since the goal is fat loss, round down to an easily measured number of 4 ounces of ground turkey.

Finally, you now know you need 5 whole eggs and 4 ounces of ground turkey for every breakfast. Now multiply both by 7 days to get what you need to plan on purchasing for the week. In this case, that amounts to 35 eggs and 28 ounces of ground turkey. In real life, purchase the amounts that are closest to what you need. If your grocery store doesn't have customizable options for ground turkey, plan on buying 2 pounds of ground turkey (32 ounces) and 3 dozen eggs (36). Those amounts now go on your grocery plan for the week.

Lunch and Dinner

Remember, we are planning on 2 protein options for Lunch and Dinner. Lunches and Dinners are often interchangeable so don't feel like you need to eat the same protein for Dinner for the whole week. You can oscillate back and forth.

Let's say this person wants chicken breast for lunch. Just like breakfast, take the amount of protein needed (67 grams) and divide it by the grams of protein in each ounce of chicken breast (9 grams). This comes out to 7.4 ounces. Round down to a more easily measured 7 ounces of chicken breast per lunch. Now multiply that by 7 days to get what you need to plan on purchasing for the week. This amount to 49 ounces of chicken breast for the week. That is an odd number so, if you can get that customized for you, great! If you can't, round to the nearest pound which, in this case, would be 3 pounds (48 ounces). That amount of chicken breast now goes on your grocery plan for the week.

This leaves poor old Top Sirloin to be counted for the dinner for the week. Once again, take the amount of protein needed (67 grams) and divide it by the grams of protein in each ounce of top sirloin (8 grams). This comes out to 8.4 ounces. Round down to a more easily measured 8 ounces of steak per dinner. Now, multiply that by 7 days to get what you need to plan on purchasing for the week. This amounts to 64 ounces of top sirloin for the week. That is exactly 4 pounds. That amount of top sirloin steak now goes on your grocery plan for the week.

Final Protein List

For our example, their final protein list for their week of food is as follows:

3 dozen eggs

2 pounds of ground turkey

3 pounds of chicken breast

4 pounds of top sirloin steak

They have now precisely planned the most important and most expensive part of their meal plan for the week.

Pro Tip*: Not all protein is created equal. Planning for variety is a necessary component for most people to stick with a particular way of eating. That being said, the costs can differ dramatically. Fresh sea food and red meat will almost always be far more costly per gram of protein than poultry or canned tuna. That does not make them bad. It is something that needs to be taken into consideration if you are working with a really tight budget. Steak can be $2.50-$5 on average per serving while Chicken can be as low as $0.50 per serving. Knowing exactly how much of a particular protein you need for the week is guaranteed to lower the cost compared to guesstimating like most people do, but steak is still more than chicken. If you need variety AND you are barely scraping by at the moment, a trick I use is to season the individual chicken portions with a different herb and/or spice. Since you can* *basically use any natural herb and spice you want to (and there are hundreds of them), you can create a lot of variety even if you can only afford one kind of protein.*

Don't let the amount of math we are about to do scare you. It may seem like a lot right now, but it gets much easier and much faster as you practice. Stick with it!

We will be following the process - Specify, Simply, Multiply, Convert.

Specify

Protein

If you don't know the numbers you need, return to the Find YOUR Serving Size section and the math you did towards the beginning of this book.

Meals Per Day ___________

Daily Grams Of Protein / Meals Per Day = Protein Serving Size

___________/ _____________=

____

Pick 2-4 Protein Sources

Meal 1

Protein Serving Size / Grams of Protein per Ounce of Protein Source = Amount of Protein Source

________________/_______________=

____

Meal 2

Protein Serving Size / Grams of Protein per Ounce of Protein Source = Amount of Protein Source

___________________/

____________________=

____

Meal 3

Protein Serving Size / Grams of Protein per Ounce of Protein Source = Amount of Protein Source

___________________/

_____________________=

____

Etc.

Simplify

Amount of Protein Source for Meal 1 —> Round Down to Nearest

Whole Number —>_______

Amount of Protein Source for Meal 2 —> Round Down to Nearest

Whole Number — >________

Amount of Protein Source for Meal 3 —> Round Down to Nearest

Whole Number — >________

Etc.

Multiply For The Week

Amount of Protein Source for Meal 1 Rounded Down x 7 =

Amount of Protein Source for Meal 2 Rounded Down x 7 =

Amount of Protein Source for Meal 3
Rounded Down x 7 =

Etc

Convert to Purchasable Amounts

Amount of Protein Source For Meal 1 For the Week Rounded to

Nearest Pound (Multiples of 16 ounces)

=_______________

Amount of Protein Source For Meal 2 For the Week Rounded to

Nearest Pound (Multiples of 16 ounces)

=_______________

Amount of Protein Source For Meal 3 For the Week Rounded to

Nearest Pound (Multiples of 16 ounces)

=_______________

Place the types of Protein and Amounts for the week on

your grocery plan. They will be under the Convert To Purchasable Amounts section.

Fats

Welcome to the land of hormone balance and energy - also known as quality fat. We are addressing this macronutrient second because it is typically the most misunderstood and miscalculated when people are trying to plan their macros. We are not answering all the questions about fat - just a few. Our main point is to help you plan it appropriately and accurately so that, whatever way of eating you are experimenting with or living in, you can be successful.

If you haven't heard already from a coworker, friend, or family member trying out the Ketogenic Diet, you're probably going to. Keto practitioners and vegans have a similar propensity for taking magnanimous (yes, the word is intentional) pride in their identity. One of the benefits of this is that more and more people are hearing the message that fat in your diet is not a bad thing. Too much fat is. The wrong type of fat is. However, good, whole food sources of fat eaten in proportion to your goals are incredibly good for your hormones, brain health, etc.

While many people are starting to understand good fats as a positive and are incorporating them in their meal plans and ways of eating, they very often miscalculate how much they are actually eating. This is usually because, while people are pretty good at figuring out how much fat is in a food that is typically seen as a fat (avocado, butter, yogurt, nuts, etc), they often forget that a large source of dietary fat comes from the meat and dairy products that we consume. For example, let's say that someone plans to eat 100 grams of fat per day. They then plan 100 grams of fat coming from avocados, nuts, and butter in their day. That's all fine and well, but if the meat that they are also eating contains 50-60 grams of fat in total, that same person may plateau or even gain weight despite believing they are following their macros. When you're planning your meals for the week, make sure to go back through the proteins you have chosen and calculate how much fat you are getting through them BEFORE you plan for other sources of fat.

Let's go back to the example of the person who needs 67 grams of fat per day in order to meet their macro experiment. That person chose eggs, ground turkey, chicken breast, and top sirloin steak as their protein sources. Since we know how much of each source they are planning on per day, it is simple to calculate how much total fat they will be ingesting through them. Once again, I will break down the amount of fat per ounce of the most common protein sources.

Chicken Breast 1g/oz Ground Turkey 3g/oz Top Sirloin Steak 4g/oz Ground Beef (85% Lean) 4g/oz 1 Whole Egg 5g/egg 1 Cup of Egg Whites 0.5g/cup

On a daily basis, our example will be eating 5 eggs, 4 ounces of ground turkey, 7 ounces of chicken, and 8 ounces of top sirloin steak. If you use the guide above, you will come up with the following totals:

5 eggs x 5 grams of fat = 25 grams of fat
4 ounces of ground turkey x 3 grams of fat = 12 grams of fat

7 ounces of chicken breast x 1 gram of fat = 7 grams of fat

8 ounces of top sirloin steak x 4 grams of fat = 32 grams of fat

Total Fat For The Day = 76 grams of fat

OH NO!!!

Things just got complicated! We are planning for 67 grams of fat but we have 76 grams of fat already in just the meat! That's an extra 81 calories!

Let's look at the good side of this first. Since the meat sources of protein already contain all the fat we need, there is no longer a need to plan to buy extra items like nuts, avocados, or real butter. That means more money in your pocket!

On the bad side, this could slow down your progress. We can approach this issue in one of two ways - accept the slightly slower rate of progress since we are still in a 400+ calorie deficit OR switch out one of the protein sources for a leaner option. Either decision is totally acceptable.

In this particular case, an easy solution would be to replace a few of the fattiest proteins (whole eggs) with a leaner alternative (egg whites). If you find yourself in this situation, a good rule of thumb is that 2 egg whites is about the same amount of protein as 1 whole egg while containing 1/10th the fat. Since the example is over by around 10 calories per day, just replace 2 of the whole eggs with 4 egg whites and the problem is solved. If you're using a carton of egg whites, that's around 1/4 cup. If you're using whole eggs and separating out the egg whites yourself, plan on buying about a dozen more for the week than originally planned.

Carbs

Finally, we close on the final macronutrient - carbohydrates. At the time of this writing, carbs are arguably the most controversial macronutrient. There are a slew of opinions on all sides from highly qualified researchers, coaches, and practitioners. The point of this book isn't to give you yet another opinion to sift through. The point of this book is to allow you to figure out what works best for YOU. Genetics, body type, activity type and level, gut biome, and your normal daily eating habits up to this point all have a large impact on how you will process carbohydrates - and that's just with the whole food sources! We want to give you a roadmap that will help you effectively experiment with amounts and types until you narrow it down to what helps you maintain your goals the best.

Despite the wide variety of opinions and responses, there are a few general principles it helps to know about your friendly neighborhood carb. Without going too deep into the weeds, the body uses the fuel that comes from carbohydrates mostly for powerful, sudden, and forceful movements. Think about helping someone lift a heavy couch, sprinting, weight lifting, martial arts, etc. This makes carbs a perfect fuel source for these activities. The more you participate in these or other similar activities, the more carbs you can use and/or handle.

Inversely, the less you participate in powerful, sudden, and forceful movements, the less carbs you can use and/or handle.

***Pro Tip**: This is not true for all people. As I've stated already, there is a lot of individual variety. We all know that one person who can seemingly eat a whole pizza, follow it with a tub of ice cream, and wash it all down with soda and never gain a pound. Odds are, if your goal is to lose weight, you are not one of those people - and that's ok. The mission is to discover what works for you - not waste time with unhelpful rants of jealousy, resentment, or frustration.*

***Pro Tip**: An interesting point about carbs is, out of the three main macronutrients, they are the least necessary for longevity, survival, or daily function. This is one reason why they are usually the easiest to manipulate for the purposes of experimentation. For most people eating at a caloric deficit for several* *months, if they hit a hard plateau, lowering carbs but keeping calories the same works for a majority of people to kickstart progress again. Once again, you need to discover what works for you. However, borrowing ideas from what works for most is a great place to start. Long story short, when you go to experiment and recalculate your macros after 4-8 weeks, the first experiment should be to lower your carb percentage, raise either protein or fat, and stick to it for another 4-8 weeks.*

Pro Tip*: A method you can look into is carb cycling. There are many different versions of carb cycling with subtle variations. However, the general idea is that you only eat carbs (or high amounts of carbs) on days (preferably around the time of day) you do a lot of intense interval training or weight lifting. On the other days (or parts of the day) you eat little to no carbs. This uses carbs to help build and repair muscle tissue more efficiently instead of being stored and creating an environment where fat storage is more likely. This is not absolutely necessary to try if you have personal or cultural considerations that would make this overly difficult. I would be amiss if I failed to clue you in on what many fitness professionals view as one of the most effective shredding techniques available.*

While fats take the title for "Most Often Miscalculated," carbs take the title for "Most Complex To Plan." I don't mean to say it's especially difficult, but there are a few points you need to keep in mind that can be easy to miss.

1. Plan Your Macros On The Wet - When you are looking up grams of carbs (I highly encourage this practice) in the food you want to use, make sure to specify 'cooked.' This is the opposite of meat - which you should measure raw. While I would like to be able to calculate everything dry to have better control of the variables, there are more resources that list cooked. We are not after perfection. We are after consistency. Ease of access to information helps with consistency.

2. Plan Your List On The Dry - There are several whole-food carb sources you may choose from and many of them expand dramatically when you prepare them - rice, beans, and quinoa are examples. If you want to prepare 1 cup of rice, just know that it only takes about 1/3 cup dry rice to do so. It will look like a very small amount when you start to prepare it and you may second guess yourself and end up putting in more. This is particularly true if you are meal prepping while hungry (which I highly recommend you don't do). Trust the process, not your eyes. Once you calculate the amount of cooked carbs you need, reverse calculate to figure out the amount of dry, pre-cooked carbs you need (see below Pro Tip for help with this). Once you figure out this number, place that type of carb and the amount you need for the week on your grocery plan.

Pro Tip: For those who are struggling with planning considering the many different water to rice ratios, there is some easy math that helps. When you have a container or bag of dry rice, look at the cooking directions on the back to see how much water is needed per cup of dry rice. After you find it, add the two numbers together to get your 'divide-by' number. Now, take the number of cups of cooked rice you need for the week and divide it by the 'divide-by' number you got earlier. This will give you how much dry rice you need to measure out for your prep. If you find yourself stuck as to how much water to use, simply multiply the amount of dry rice you are measuring by the original amount of water needed per cup of dry rice.

Example:

Let's assume you need 14 cups of cooked rice prepared for the week. We are going to look at three different scenarios.

Rice 1 needs 3 cups of water per 1 cup of dry rice. Add the two measurements together to get your 'divide-by' number - 4. Since you need 14 cups of cooked rice, divide 14 by 4 to get how much dry rice you need to measure out - 3.5 cups dry rice. Now multiply that number by the original 3 cups of water to get how much water you need to use -10.5 cups of water.

Rice 2 needs 2 cups of water per 1 cup of dry rice. Add the two measurements together to get your 'divide-by' number -

3. Since you need 14 cups of cooked rice, divide 14 by 3 to get how much dry rice you need to measure out - 4.67 (4 and 2/3s) cups dry rice. Now multiply that number by the original 2 cups of water to get how much water you need to use - 9.33 (9 and 1/3) cups of water.

Rice 3 needs 1.5 cups of water per 1 cup of rice. Add the two measurements together to get your 'divide-by' number - 2.5. Since you need 14 cups of cooked rice, divide 14 by 2.5 to get how much dry rice you need to measure out - 5.6 cups dry rice. Now multiply that number by the original 1.5 cups of water to get how much water you need to use - 8.4 cups of water (you can round to 8.5 cups of water to make it easier).

Calculating YOUR Serving Size

Just as with the protein, your serving size of carbs depends on how many grams of carbs you are planning for per day and how many meals you can stick to per day. It also matters whether or not they will be doing a version of carb cycling. We will look at both.

First, let's assume this person wants to keep all meals balanced and have a source of carbs at every meal. Staying consistent with our example, let's say this person is planning for 150 grams of carbs per day and they can eat 3 times per day. 150 grams of carbs divided by 3 meals per day equals 50 grams of carbs per meal. I will list some of the most common carb sources and their grams of carbs per unit of measurement as a guide. For individually small carb sources such as rice, beans, and quinoa, I have found it easier to use cups as a standard of measurement since they fit fully and easily. For individually larger carb sources such as white potatoes, sweet potatoes, or fruit, I have found it easier to use ounces as a standard of measurement, very similar to how we measure meat.

White Potato = 5g/ounce

Sweet Potato = 6g/ounce Yams = 8g/ounce Oats = 30g/cup Rice = 53g/cup Quinoa = 32g/cup

For simplest prep, pick 2-3 sources of carbs for the week and begin the calculations. Let's say this person wants to eat Sweet Potato and Oats for their carbs for the week.

Meal 1

This person wants oatmeal (the kind where oats is the only ingredient) for breakfast all 7 days. Take the Amount of Carbs Needed Per Meal (50), and divide it by the number of grams of carbs in 1 cup of cooked oats (30g). When you do so, you will get 1.67 (1 and 2/3s) cups of cooked oats needed per day. Multiply that by the days in the week (7) and you will find you need a total of 11.67 (11 and 2/3s) cups of cooked oats for the week.

In this case, find out the amount of water needed per cup of dry oats for your particular brand and follow the math on the previous Pro Tip to find out how much dry oats you should plan on purchasing. Now put this type of carb and amount needed on your grocery plan for the week.

Pro Tip: *Carbs are often the cheapest part of the macro*

plan and they often can only be purchased in minimum quantities which far exceed what most people need in a week. To counter this, calculate what you need for the week and see if you can squeeze in an uncooked supply that lasts you 2-4 weeks.

Meals 2 and 3

This person loves sweet potato so they want to have it for both lunch and dinner.

Since they want it for both meals, you can combine the numbers together - 50 grams of carbs per meal x 2 meals = 100 total grams of carbs for lunch and dinner. Now take the total daily need and divide it by the amount of carb grams per ounce of sweet potato - 100 grams of needed carbs / 6g per ounce for sweet potato = 16.67 (16 and 2/3s) ounces of sweet potato needed daily. As you may have noticed, this is slightly more than 1 pound (16 ounces). Since the goal is fat loss, round down to the nearest pound.

Multiply that by 7 days in order to plan what they need for the week - 7 pounds of sweet potato. Now put this type of carb and amount needed on your grocery plan for the week.

Carb Cycling

There are many ways to do carb cycling, but one of the simplest forms is simply to plan to eat most, if not all, of your carbs for the day for the meal/s closest to your workout. If this is the way you want to plan to eat your carbs, the process is identical. The only difference is that, instead of breaking it down to individual meals spread throughout the day, you can simply divide your total carb intake for the day and divide it by the grams of carbs in your chosen carb source. That will give you what you need to consume right around your workout.

Now You Try.

Carbs Needed for the Day / Meals Per Day = Carbs Per Meal

_________________/
____________=_____________

Carbs Per Meal / Grams of Carbs Per Unit of Measurement = Amount of Carb
Type Needed Per Meal

_________________/
____________=_____________

Amount of Carb Type Needed Per Meal x 7 Days = Amount of Carb Type Needed For The Week

_____________ x 7 Days =

____

Repeat for each meal. Place both type and amount of carbs needed for the week on your grocery plan.

Vegetables

Unless you are training for a physique show where every calorie counts, for the purposes of daily life, vegetables are a freebie. That's right! You can have as many vegetables as you want! The only vegetables I recommend avoiding if you are getting all the carbs you need from other sources are squash, pumpkin, and other varieties of gourd. They tend to be higher in carbs and calories. However, if you are avoiding carbs from other sources, these particular vegetables can be a good carb source. They are not a freebie and should not be counted as such. Instead, focus on varieties of color and dark green vegetables - broccoli, kale, spinach, bell peppers, beets, radishes, mustard greens, etc. If you can't program these into every meal, program them in for at least 1-2 meals.

Why are they so important if you already have your main macros? While planning your macros is a great way to lose excess fat, gain muscle, or maintain your physique goal, it doesn't cover everything about health. As important as macronutrients are, micronutrients (vitamins, minerals, fiber, etc) are also incredibly important.

As an analogy, imagine that you spent a lot of time working on the engine of a car - upgrading it's horsepower, upgrading the quality of fuel, making sure it runs effectively - but never changed the oil or flushed the transmission fluid. You can upgrade and take care of that engine all you want, but if you ignore the "little stuff," eventually that engine will come to a screeching halt.

The micronutrients you ingest from vegetables help you maintain clean energy, help keep your gut microbiome fed, ensure you get quality fiber, keep your cells running efficiently, and, overall, do a lot to keep your body operating at optimum health. Ignore them at your own peril.

Pro Tip: *We will be discussing how to prepare vegetables so that they stay fresh for several days. However, if you simply cannot bear to eat a crown of broccoli, there are alternatives. Greens powders are* *basically a compilation of dozens of vegetables which are then dehydrated and blended into a powder. They act as nutritional insurance just in case the day doesn't go perfectly as planned. Whether you can stomach vegetables or not, a scoop of greens powder gives you the comfort of knowing you have at least the majority of micronutrients you need. Furthermore, even a powder that is more on the expensive side ($45-$60 for a month's supply) still only amounts to $1.50-$2 per day for a day's worth of vegetables. If you can do both, that's perfect. If you're working with an extra tight budget, sometimes the greens powder will give you the best bang for your buck and is the better choice.*

***Pro Tip**: As an average, vegetables lose about 20% of their weight when you peel the skin, cut off the stalks, etc. Therefore, if you want to plan for eating, for example, 1/2 pound of vegetables per day (8 ounces), you need to divide the weight of vegetables you want by 0.8 in order to calculate the weight of vegetables you actually need to purchase.*

***Example:** Let's say you want to eat 1/2 (0.5) pounds of vegetables per day in order to get 4 ounces of vegetables for two meals per day. Get a calculator and divide the amount you want to eat in total (0.5 pounds) by 80% (0.8) in order to capture the weight of vegetables* *you need to plan on purchasing. In this example, 0.5 / 0.8 = 0.625 pounds per day. Next, multiply this number by 7 days in order to discover the total weight you need to buy for the week. In this example, 0.625 pounds x 7 days = 4.375 pounds of vegetables for the week. To make it easier, round up to the nearest half pound. In this example, 4.375 pounds —> 4.5 pounds of raw vegetables.*

If you choose to eat vegetables (my recommendation) over getting a greens powder, put 1-4 vegetables on your grocery plan and make sure to notate the total weight you need to purchase (see above). Once you get to the grocery store, simply weigh and add up the weight of the vegetables you choose until you reach the total weight you are going for. If you haven't figured it out yet, grocery stores and hand-held calculators work really well together when you are trying to eat healthy for as little as possible. Precision is the key.

Execute The Grocery Plan

"A lot of potential and no potential have the same result if no action is taken."

~Life Observation~

Based on the work from the previous sections, you should now have your grocery plan for the week with all of your protein sources, fat sources, carb sources, and vegetables as well as the amounts you need of each. It is now time to go to the grocery store.

Going to the grocery store without a specific plan is the number one mistake people can make when they are trying to eat towards their goals with a low income. I have tested this with myself and it still stands true. I have been eating at least 95% clean for many years. I don't get fast food. I don't buy junk food. I steer clear of over-processed foods. The aisles in a grocery store generally hold no appeal for me. Having practiced this for so long, I should be able to go into the grocery store with a general idea of what I need and walk out getting only what I need. In fact, when I do convince myself that this is feasible, I am quickly reminded that it is always a bad idea.

When I go in without a plan, I always spend $50-$100 more for a week of food than I spend if I go in with a plan. I have been shopping successfully with a plan for years. You might think that, if anyone can walk into a store without a plan, shop for the week, and come out without spending too much, it would be me. Surprisingly, that is incorrect. I grew up poor and have worked with thousands of clients who grew up poor. I know that this is one sneaky area which keeps people poorer than they need to be while preventing them from consistently eating good, real food. While "healthy" drive-thru options are highly overpriced, going in to a grocery store planning to eat healthy but without a plan on what exactly you need to purchase is a sure-fire way to at least double what you had planned on spending. Why is this the case?

To be fair, this could be due to a variety of emotional and psychological underpinnings. Few external things are as connected to our psychology as our food. However, there is also another, more nefarious, reason why you spend more without a plan. Get ready to get upset.

If you are going into a grocery store, even with a plan, you need to realize that you are entering into an epicenter for marketing and advertising. I am not exaggerating when I state that every single aisle represents millions of dollars of research and testing and the brightest minds in sales, marketing, and psychology. These millions of dollars and hundreds of bright minds are all funneled in to one thing - catching your eye and getting you to put a particular product in your cart. Imagine trying to play chess with a hundred chess masters at the same time without a plan or cogent strategy on how to win. It doesn't matter how intelligent you are, you are going to lose. It is nearly impossible to shop accurately and inexpensively based on what you 'feel' or 'think' you need when you are being accosted on all sides by brilliant marketers who have designed every letter, claim, font, and picture to be maximally effective and psychologically appealing towards a purchase as possible. A great starting strategy to help win a battle is to avoid walking alone straight into the front lines of the enemy.

With the above being said, that is why it is incredibly important, especially for those who are broke, to enter the grocery store with a very specific list and a commitment to buy ONLY what is on that list. While having a specific list of types and amounts of food does not make you bullet-proof to the marketers, it does make you much more bullet-resistant.

Pro Tip: Try and set a speed record. Refuse to enter a grocery store without your specific plan. Once you have it, go the store and try to get in and out of the store in the fastest time possible. I encourage you to time yourself. This fun element of self-competition, combined with your specific grocery plan, will make it a lot easier to stick to the food that will help you reach your goals all while costing you as little as possible. Your wallet will be happy you read this. (My record is 7 minutes)

Pro Tip: Many grocery stores in modern times allow you to order your groceries online and arrange for them to drop it off or for you to pick it up. At the time of this writing, these services were either free or cost as little as $5 per time. Why would we spend extra money for this service? Isn't that for rich people? The whole point of taking advantage of this service is to minimize the chance that you will make an impulse purchase. As I said before, as healthy and cost-conscious as I am, I still spend $50-$100 on average MORE for a week of food thanks to impulse purchases of "health" food IF I don't bring a specific grocery plan. If you attempt grocery planning for several weeks and, despite your grocery plan and all your intentions, you still find yourself impulse spending on as little as 2 products, I can almost guarantee that it will be cheaper to hire someone to do the shopping for you.

Organic vs. Non-organic

Before we move on to the meal- prepping strategy section, I am going to address a question/concern I hear all the time - Organic or Non-organic? That is the question. After all, if you're going to be healthy, shouldn't you go all the way?

That is a fair question. However, *caveat emptor,* my friend. I am actually saddened to say this (I fell for it too, at first), but the label 'Organic' doesn't actually mean much. I am certain there are farms and ranches that put 'Organic' on their labels because it actually means something - no toxic pesticides, antibiotics, hormones, grass-fed AND finished, etc. However, there are quite a few holes in the regulations which can result in the word 'Organic' being on a product while still containing non-organic, potentially harmful materials - and that's assuming all regulations are being followed and enforced. According to the USDAs guide for Organic Crop Producers (yes, I read it) there are three different labels for three different levels of organic when it comes to plant-based products and vegetables.

1. "100 Percent Organic" is the only label said to guarantee that every process and ingredient in the

product is fully organic from start to finish.

2. “Organic” can be used as a label if a product contains at least 95% organic ingredients. That means 5% of your product is allowed to be something else.

3. “Made with Organic ______ ” can be used to label a product that contains at least 70% organically produced ingredients. This means almost a third of your product (30%) can have nonorganic ingredients and/or additives and still have the word ‘Organic’ on it.

“Organic” meat is a whole other animal (pun intended). You may have noticed some products which proudly proclaim ‘Grass-Fed’ on their label. Well, that particular label only needs proof that the animals have eaten grass for a period of time - NOT their whole lives. ‘Organic, Grass-Fed’ only needs proof that 30 percent of the animal’s food was grass - leaving 70 percent open to question. Even ‘Pasture-Raised’ contains enough holes in its legal definition to effectively dilute any certainty that the animal was fed only quality food, lived in an unstressful environment, or has any real health benefits to justify the price being 2-5 times higher. The only way to know for sure is to actually know the farmer or rancher themselves. If you have the opportunity to get to know your organic farmer and rancher, by all means, do it! For many, that isn't feasible in the moment.

Don't misunderstand my intent to be negative. The initial goal of the organic label is noble, the requirements can be extensive, and farmers and ranchers work really hard to be able to call their produce and products 'Organic.' However, not all farms are noble and there is such a wide range of definitions for what it means that, in some ways, 'Organic' loses its meaning.

Why does this matter to you? Because many people who are trying to eat healthier choose pricey "health" food with the word 'Organic' on it and end up paying 2-5 times the normal amount for something that could very well have little to no difference in actual quality and safety. A huge majority of people have no idea that there is a massive difference between "Made with Organic" and "100 Percent Organic." A huge majority of people have no idea that labels such as 'Natural' or 'Grass-Fed' on meat products essentially mean nothing. All they see is the word 'Organic' somewhere on the label and they immediately assume that it is extra healthy and worth the much higher price point. A few trips to the grocery store to get ‘Organic’ food is usually all it takes to convince someone that they will have to wait to improve their body and health because “eating healthy is too expensive.”

Unless you personally know the farmer and their process or come across a “100 Percent Organic” label, there isn’t a surefire way to know that this food you are about to spend 2-5 times more than normal on is actually that much healthier than the normal meat and produce. Don’t get me wrong. I love the idea of organic. I get ‘Grass-Fed, Grass-Finished’ beef and ‘Pasture-Raised’ eggs when I have a few extra dollars I can legitimately spare. However, when finances are tight, choosing real, whole foods is still very doable and inexpensive - shopping ‘organic’ is often not. A year consistently eating real food, even if it isn’t organic, is far more healthy than going full organic if it will only leave you with an empty wallet and no motivation to continue. The consistent average will always beat the inconsistent perfect.

Prepare The Meals

You've done it! You've done all the calculations, created your list, stuck to that list, stood in shock for a moment as you see a price tag significantly lower than normal (gotta love precise shopping), and have returned to your lair to begin the magic of meal prepping.

This final step can be a huge obstacle for many people. We've already busted the myth that eating healthy is too expensive. The myth that it takes too much time and that food just goes to waste is still standing. This section will kill that myth once and for all so you can quickly, cheaply, and freely pursue your goals. With the right organization and process, you can spend less than an hour (clean-up included) preparing food for the whole week and around a minute every morning. That's less time than a single restaurant visit or a handful of drive-thru experiences!

There are many methods of prepping and I encourage you to experiment with them as time goes on - just to keep it interesting. However, the methods I am about to divulge are designed to be the sweet spot of simple, fast, and good-tasting all while keeping food fresh all week long. I have been using this method myself for several years and have the steps down to a science. I can confidently state that if someone were to order a single meal of take-out, or even delivery, at the same time I start prepping for the whole week, I can almost guarantee that I will have food ready to go, properly stored, and the kitchen cleaned before UberEats or Door Dash even reach their door. With enough time and practice, you will be able to say the same.

Now for the fun part.

The key to this method is organization. First, make sure you have all the materials you need ready to go and easily accessible. Searching for these items in the middle of prepping throws off the flow of movement, wastes time, introduces frustration, and generally contributes to a bad experience. The materials you will need are as follows:

Pot

Baking Sheet Colander/ Strainer Cutting Board Aluminum Foil Knife

Stirring/ Serving Utensil Meat Thermometer

Gallon Zip-Loc Bags Tupperware 2 Timers

When deciding how to cook your meals, remember that the goal is to make this as simple and quick as possible without sacrificing palatability (taste). The more variables and movements your plan requires, the more likely preparation will take longer than expected and result in subpar food. It's difficult to keep from burning the rice when constant attention needs to be paid to grilling the chicken and you still haven't touched the vegetables and the dishes are piling up and you forgot to set the timer and your phone keeps going off and...you get the point. Simple and long is always faster than complicated and quick. Thus, this method is designed to minimize the time you are actively working on any one component of food and allowing you to focus on the task at hand.

The first food group that needs to be cooked are your meats. My preferred method of preparing all meats is baking. There are a few reasons for this.

Firstly, baking requires very minimal steps on your part. Preheat, prep the meat, set the timer, and leave it alone until the timer goes off. This is much easier than grilling which requires minute by minute attention. Any food you have to babysit is taking time and attention from other parts of the meal.

Secondly, baking sheets and ovens are much larger than the heating surface on a stovetop. This means you can cook more meat at the same time than is typically possible if you grill.

Thirdly, it takes a lot less of your time. The amount of time it takes to preheat the oven, prep the meat, set the timer, and put it in the oven can be as little as 5 minutes. Add 3 more minutes for checking the temperature and dishing out the meat at the end and you can prepare an entire week's worth of meat with only 8 minutes of your time. Even if the meat is in the oven for 45 minutes, 40 of those minutes are free for you to prepare the carbs, cut and prep the vegetables, and clean. Contrast this with grilling which often requires constant attention while you constantly have to bounce back and forth between making the other parts of your meals and checking on the grilling.

Furthermore, very rarely can you grill all of the meat at the same time due to limits on the size of the pans and room on the stovetop. This means you have to grill the meat a few pieces at a time. This can easily take 2040 minutes and highly limits your ability to focus on other parts of the meal prep which increases your likelihood of mistakes and greatly increases the total time you take.

Prepping the meat is fairly simple. Using chicken breast as an example (though this will work for almost any meat), preheat the oven to 350 degrees. While it is preheating, place each piece (cut to approximately a single serving size) on an individual portion of aluminum foil, dust with whichever herb and spice suits your fancy, wrap the individual chicken portion in the aluminum foil and place on the baking sheet. Repeat until all of the chicken has been prepared and placed on the baking sheet. Typically, you can get this done before the oven finishes preheating.

Pro Tip: If you don't have a scale yet or don't have time to measure at any point, there is a different way. The key is to not be obsessed with exact amounts. Get as close as possible but don't stress about slight deviations. Remember, the consistent average is a much better, easier, simpler, and faster metric to use. As long as your days and weeks look relatively the same across the board from a nutritional standpoint, it doesn't really matter whether a few meals are off by an ounce or two. For example, let's say that your calculations show you need 4 ounces of ground beef as a serving per meal. Ground beef is sold by the pound (16 ounces). If you don't have the time or equipment to measure everything out, simply separate the ground beef into four equal-looking portions (16 ounces of beef / 4 ounces per meal = 4 servings) and wrap them up. The same idea works for items such as chicken.

You should be able to do all of this in minutes. This allows time to wash your hands and begin measuring out the carbohydrates. When the oven is preheated, place the baking sheet in the oven and set your first timer to 45 minutes (This is for thicker chicken breast. Thinner chicken breast should reach the recommended temperature of 165 degrees Fahrenheit after 35-40 minutes).

This method will work with almost all meats and will ensure they are all fully cooked. You can even bake multiple kinds of meat at the same time. Simply cut your two to three options into the correct serving size for you based on the type of meat, wrap each serving individually, and follow the same guidelines as above.

Note: Because the meat portions are individually and fully wrapped in aluminum foil, letting the meat stay in the oven for several extra minutes will not actually burn it. You have created a bunch of mini-pressure cookers so, if anything, the meat gets even more tender if you let it stay in the oven a little "too long."

Pro Tip: You should keep the meat in the aluminum foil when you put it into your protein container in the refrigerator. This will allow it to avoid oxygen exposure, keep from drying out, and is simply faster than unwrapping them unnecessarily.to remove the foil before you microwave it - Please.

Just remember

Once you get the protein in the oven, you now have your hands free to focus on prepping your carbs - assuming you are using them.

If you are using carbs such as sweet potatoes, then you can boil them along with the meat for around the same amount of time.

If you're using carbs that need water such as rice, lentils, or beans they simply need measured out, washed (using the strainer or colander), placed in the appropriate amount of water, brought to a quick boil, and then immediately set to a slow simmer until ready. The preparation, to include measuring, washing, boiling, and setting to simmer, should take no more than 10 minutes. If you do this immediately after putting the meat in the oven, this means that you can have most of the work done for proteins and carbs in

15 minutes and need only minimal monitoring thereafter until they're finished.

After you have prepped the proteins and carbs and set them on their way, it is now time to prep the vegetables.

First, slice and dice them to your preference while still raw. It is after this point where most meal preppers fail miserably. Both oxygen and moisture exposure accelerate the spoiling of all foods, but especially vegetables - broccoli is particularly unforgiving. If you proceed to steam your vegetables, you are dooming them to be spoiled and unpalatable in three days AT THE MOST. This can, and often does, result in at least half of the vegetables (and even meals as a whole) going to waste or, if you manage to choke them down then....well, you're choking them down. To avoid this, there are two very simple solutions.

1. Break the vegetables up into three even piles. Store two piles raw in a Ziploc bag in the refrigerator

(make sure to squeeze the air out). Steam the other third for the first two days of the week and simply remember to steam the vegetables in the fridge on the third day and fifth day for the rest of the week.

2. Store ALL of the vegetables raw in a Ziploc bag in the refrigerator (Make Sure To Squeeze The Air Out). Each morning, divvy out a portion of the vegetables into the Tupperware of the day and return the remainder to the refrigerator (MAKE SURE TO SQUEEZE THE AIR OUT). Believe me, if you've ever had the opportunity to smell five-day-old steamed broccoli or spinach and kale after a week of air exposure, you understand how important this is for your senses. Meals shouldn't come with a gag reflex. If you are reheating your meals via microwave, by leaving the lid on while heating, the trapped and heated moisture from the proteins and carbs will actually steam the vegetables for you. If you choose the second option, the preparation for the vegetables can take anywhere from 2-6 minutes. If you choose the first option, it can take up to 15 minutes. Worst case scenario, most of the work for the meal prep can be done in 30 minutes or less.

Don't be a slacker. If you have time to lean, you have time to clean. If you have ever worked in a restaurant environment, then this phrase might bring back some unpleasant memories. However, it is still true. Particularly after a few weeks of practice, you can end up getting so efficient at meal prepping that you can spend half the time reading or on your phone. While your efficiency is laudable, it is no good if the process still takes an extra hour because you left all the clean-up until the end. Everything is already on a timer, so you don't have to worry about anything until the timer goes off. Until then, utilize the time to wash the dishes, fill the dishwasher, wipe the counters down, and pull out the containers you are going to fill. The fifteen minutes from the time you finish prepping the vegetables to the time the proteins have finished can drastically reduce end of prep clean-up time, if not eliminate it almost completely.

Buffet Method

If you have looked at the standard meal prep pictures that plaster the pages of social media everywhere, you'll notice that, for the most part, they all look relatively similar - each individual meal is prepared to eat as is. While this looks great on Instagram, it can cause a few problems as the days go on.

Believe it or not, the second most common reason healthy eating is seen as so expensive is that such a large proportion goes to waste and must be thrown away because it goes bad before the week runs out. To make matter worse, if one part of the meals goes bad, it spoils the rest of the meal as well. Because of this, it is very easy to end up throwing out a couple day's worth of food and having to resort to ordering that pizza or stopping by the deli just to eat.

Beyond the waste, lost food, lost money, and lost time, the experience of opening up a Tupperware container to discover spoiled food inside can be quite visceral - by which I mean that the urge to vomit the moment the putrid stench slams into your nostrils is very real and not an experience you want to repeat. Despite the unpleasantness of this, I used to experience this several times over the course of a few months. Days 1 -3 would typically be great, but Days 4-6 would vacillate between doable and terrible. This meant I had to start meal- prepping twice a week instead of once a week just to keep things edible, almost doubling my kitchen time and making it increasingly difficult to sustain.

While there are those who are able to make this work, I needed to find a different way. I experimented with a few different strategies and finally settled on what I call the Buffet Method. It's designed to mitigate spoiling risk, cross contamination, and eliminate the need to throw away the whole meal if only part of it goes bad. Instead of making the meals ready-to-eat, you make and store each part of the meals separately and compile them in the container/s for the day each morning (takes less time than even the fastest drive-thru).

If the bag with the vegetables goes bad quicker than expected, you still have your carbs and proteins left unspoiled and ready to go. How does this work? Simply have a single container for each category and type of food. If you make three days of turkey and three days of chicken, have one container for all the turkey and another container for all the chicken.

For vegetables, instead of using Tupperware, it is especially important to use some form of a Zip-loc bag. Food spoils through a variety of means, but the fastest is oxidation. The more oxygen your food is exposed to, the faster it will spoil. This is especially true of vegetables. The fastest, simplest, and cheapest way to avoid this is to place all of the cut, but uncooked, vegetables in a Zip-loc bag, close it almost all the way, press on the bag to squeeze all the air out possible, and then finish closing it. Keeping the vegetables fresh and uncooked will greatly increase the amount of time they remain unspoiled. Sealing them in a Zip-loc bag with all the air squeezed out can keep them tasting (and smelling) just as fresh on Day 6 as they did on Day 1. For this same reason, if you are able to individually wrap each serving of protein in aluminum foil, this will extend the number of days the meat tastes great and is safe to eat.

For carbohydrates, place each type in its own Tupperware container. As long as they are not stored with excess water, they tend to remain quite palatable with no extra steps needed.

Individuation - What To Do From Here

Now you have it! You've got the system in your hand. If you've been used to eating junk food and overly-processed meals for years, you're about to have an incredible month. The extra pounds are going to start melting away. Your energy levels are going to be noticeably higher. Your ability to focus, and sustain that focus, will increase. Your stress levels are about to go down and your joy levels are about to go up. Some of you will be satisfied. A lot of you may still have this nagging question about whether this system is the best for you as an individual. Honestly, if you've gotten this far, this is where you can release your inner (or outer) nerd and really start the process of tweaking and experimenting with what works best for you. The following pages will focus on how to make the adjustments until you find the absolute best plan for you.

One of the key benefits to having a baseline format in which you plan, prepare, and consume your food is that it allows you to do exactly what any scientist (mad or otherwise) tries to do in their experiments - isolate the variables. You've already taken a big step towards health by simply switching to eating real food as a rule. The next step is to discover what types and ratios of food get you (and keep you) where you want to be.

Start with the baseline calories and macros you calculated at the beginning of this book. Think of your meal prepping design as a set of four-week experiments. If your positive results are steady, stay the course for another four weeks. Remember, just because results slow down, does not mean that your meal prep strategy is no longer working.

It is very common for the first few weeks of any routine or regimen to be those with the most drastic progress, particularly when you used to have no regimen or routine whatsoever. However, if the progress seems to become painfully slow or even stop, it may be time to start changing some of the variables in your meal planning.

The first point of experimentation is to have an idea of which variables are the most likely to cause a positive change in results. Of the four variables - protein, carbohydrates, vegetables, fats - changing the amount of protein per meal to be higher or lower is the least likely to cause a substantial change in fat loss. While it could have a moderate effect, it won't have nearly the near-term effect on fat loss that the other variables will.

Alongside protein, vegetable intake should also not be lowered. For those of you who know a thing or two about food types, you may have already cringed at the fact that I placed vegetables and carbohydrates as two separate categories. While vegetables are clearly a source of carbohydrates, they deserve their own category for two reasons, 1) the actual amount of carbohydrates within non-starchy vegetables is very minimal and 2) their primary value is as a rich source of micronutrients.

Micronutrients are all those little but vital vitamins and minerals that help the body run effectively, efficiently, and healthily like beta-carotene, thiamin, riboflavin, vitamin C and many others. Decreasing vegetable intake is very unlikely to result in positive results. Increasing vegetable intake, while certainly not harmful, will not likely result in much better results if all the other variables remain the same. To make a long explanation short, keep the greens and the proteins the same. Expend your initial efforts on playing with the ratios of carbohydrates and fats.

A good first experiment is to keep everything the same amount and, instead, experiment with colors. For example, if you have been using white carbohydrates such as potatoes and rice, trying switching to other-colored carbohydrates like lentils, beans, and sweet potatoes. This change alone can often dramatically improve results.

Pro Tip: One thing to keep in mind when experimenting with carbohydrates and fats is that they do not have the same amount of calories. If you decrease carbs by 2 ounces on average, that does not mean you increase fats by 2 ounces. Fat has 9 calories per gram while carbs have 4 calories per gram. So if you decrease carbs by 2 ounces, you should increase fats by 1 ounce to replace the energy lost with the decrease in carbs. If you cut out carbs completely (experimenting with a ketogenic diet), you should start with around 3 ounces of fat per meal and then taper up if, after several days, you still find your energy levels are low.

Another thing to keep in mind is that carbs, as helpful as they are in providing quick stores of energy, particularly for lifting weights, are not as vital to the human body as fats are. Cutting out bad fats - fried foods, corn oil, fake dairy, etc. - is always a good idea. Cutting out all fats is never a good idea.

The Joy of Experimentation

There are two specific reasons that learning to experiment with your food is very important. Firstly, it puts you in charge of your food choices. You are taking a proactive approach to how you view, plan, and consume your food instead of allowing food to be a reactionary choice driven by a lack of time or whatever you're craving in the moment.

Fast food establishments and grocery stores are not only set up to quickly satisfy bad cravings, but also to create those cravings. Did you think it was accidental that the bakery is always right by the entrance to any grocery store? Store owners know the effect that the smell of freshly baked bread has on the minds and emotions of shoppers. Even if they don't end up getting bread, the scent alone incites cravings and almost guarantees the unwary shopper will purchase a few extra items accordingly.

When food becomes something you proactively plan in order to meet your goals instead of something you react with when you feel stress, a craving, or mild hunger, you begin to take control of a huge part of life. Your relationship to food changes to become a tool in your hand instead of yet another point of pain and frustration. Experimenting takes it to yet another level of control that adds a bit of fun to the process and helps to keep things interesting.

Experimentation also adds a little self-discovery. Instead of falling sway to the seemingly constant changes in diet advice popping up online and on television, you are figuring out what works for you in a clearer, more controlled way. Trying different diets and supplements is a hit or miss game, but a lot more miss. Each attempt ends with the "magic" diet or supplement not working after only a few weeks or, even worse, working but being impossible to sustain (I've heard of things as crazy as eating nothing more than one cabbage and one potato a day). By understanding, controlling, and adjusting the variables yourself, you begin to have an inherent understanding of what works with your own body that doesn't require spending thousands upon thousands of dollars over the years trying all the new programs on the market.

Just as no workout program will fit everyone, no diet program will fit everyone. Trying all of them will simply be exhausting and demotivating. It is much better to use basic principles, simple variables, and easy to track changes in those variables to learn what really works best for you. A craftsman that has mastered the use of five tools will always beat a weekend warrior who is always buying another tool and doesn't really know how to use any of them.

As a bonus benefit, experimenting with the use of a few simple principles and a few simple variables gives you a solid baseline to which you can always return while also providing the flexibility to try any sort of dieting style you want to. Most of the time, when a diet proves ineffective or unsustainable, the reaction is to return to a style of eating that is awful - whether that be binging on ice cream, pizza, and candy or simply eating without regard to what helps you or hurts you. Why? Because, to a lesser extreme, that is often the baseline style of eating you were used to before you tried the diet. You are set up to fail if you don't completely succeed. But if your baseline style of eating still follows the principles of health and has a default setting of variables, then that will be what you return to if an experiment doesn't work out well. What does that mean? It means that even when you fail, you're set up to win. In a game involving just yourself, there shouldn't be a loser.

Final Really Helpful Tips

"Cheat" Day and the Language Game

Now we come to the question that has probably been nagging you - what about cheat day? If you've spent any time hanging around fitness people, reading over fitness blogs, or watching fitness channels on YouTube, you have inevitably heard of this enticing concept called a "Cheat Day." While it sounds great, it can be a stumbling block to derail your progress in more ways than one - and not the way you think.

The whole concept of a cheat day centers around language stating that food is either 'Good' or 'Bad.' Thus, when you divulge yourself in a slice of pizza at a family get together, you can end up fighting a sense of shame that you are cheating on your diet. That's problematic for a few reasons.

First, 'Good' and 'Bad' are words describing value and morality - neither of which apply to a slice of pizza. You are not 'Bad' when you eat a pizza anymore than you are 'Good' when you eat broccoli. Food is fuel and medicine - not a sermon. Instead of using words like 'Good' and 'Bad,' use more accurate descriptions like 'Helpful' and 'Unhelpful.'

Second, when you call something a “Cheat” meal - the implicit assumption is that you are “cheating” on your diet. That makes no sense! If you are choosing to follow a specific way of eating, the whole point is to serve YOU and help YOU achieve the goals YOU have set your heart and mind on. You owe a particular ‘diet’ nothing. It’s there to serve you.

You’re not there to serve it. Bring the focus back on the person - You - and ask yourself, ”Is this food serving me or is this dragging me down?” “Is this helpful or unhelpful to what I want to do?” Keep the focus on you and your goals - not a set of rules lording over you.

Third, shame language leads to self-pity. Self-pity can lead to choosing more unhelpful foods precisely BECAUSE they are unhelpful. That’s why ‘cheat’ meals often turn into ‘cheat’ days and spiral into a ‘bad’ week and a weak commitment to get back on the wagon Monday. If you are trying to lose excess fat and you eat a few slices of pizza at a friend’s house, acknowledge that those slices weren’t helpful (but without the judgment of words like ‘bad’ and ‘cheat’) and look to choose something helpful next time you eat. In fact, there may even be times when food which would normally be unhelpful can actually be helpful. It's a spectrum that adjusts to the context.

Fourth, change the language of 'cheat' meals into 'treat' meals. In the times where it is actually fully appropriate and helpful to eat something which is typically unhelpful, acknowledge those times as 'treat' meals - something you have no need to feel bad for at all. Treat meals are done with intention and are typically planned ahead of time. Cheat meals are typically reactive and are done with a twinge of regret. Choose the helpful method.

Breakfast

If you are struggling to make a good breakfast in the morning and find yourself often rushing off to work or school with nothing in your stomach, then you already know the struggles of hunger that hit you a few hours later and make it very difficult to stay on course. Here are three breakfast strategies that can help.

1) Set your alarm clock for twenty to thirty minutes prior to your normal waking time.

If you are in a rush every morning, chances are

that you aren't getting up early enough. How you start your day can set the tone for your day. It's rarely a good idea to set the tone of the day being rushed and frazzled. An extra twenty to thirty minutes of morning time before you head off for the day can do wonders to help slow things down, get more mentally and emotionally collected, and actually have time to whip up a quick and nutrition-packed breakfast to prevent future unnecessary hunger pangs. While the first few days of waking up earlier will be rough, the stress it can relieve and prevent throughout the whole day more than makes up for it.

2) Prepare the breakfast the night before.

I am not a morning person. The last thing on my mind when I wake up, whether it's five minutes late or an hour early, is making breakfast. After many attempts at changing this fact about me, I finally decided to work around it. I don't typically prefer to take in very many supplements, but this is the one point where I decided that a protein shake helps. A bit before I go to bed, I will make a simple protein shake and store it in the refrigerator overnight. The next morning, when I am trying to collect my thoughts into some type of coherence, all I have to do is open the refrigerator and grab my breakfast.

3) Try intermittent fasting

For some people, eating in the morning is simply not going to happen. Rather than see it as a failure that dooms you, try out intermittent fasting for four weeks and see if it fits your lifestyle a bit better. While the literature on fasting is vast, the basic idea is that if you limit the window of time in the day that you can eat to 8 hours or less (some go as far as to only eat one meal a day), you can afford to eat more during your meals and the consistency of the window of time is more important than the timing of the window. What this means is that it doesn't matter when the eating window starts as long as it starts at the same time every day. So if you cannot eat breakfast to save your life, perhaps having an eating window that doesn't start until 12 PM and always ends by 8 PM will suit your lifestyle better.

When Things Don't Go As Planned

It's inevitable. You ate your breakfast, packed your lunch, set off on your day feeling extra prepared. Mid-day comes around and you eat your packed lunch, feeling the gratification that comes with eating in a way that helps you move forward. Then, it hits you. Three hours later something happens that derails your plans for the day and it will be another four hours before you can get back home. An intense and incredibly distracting hunger seemingly storms you out of nowhere. You have no food left and the only options around are sugary snacks, fake food, or fast food. You might be able to power through the hunger to the end of the day, but the odds are stacked against you. A quick detour from your plan and you may feel like you have “ruined” your diet. Feeling like you failed, it is easy to tell yourself that you’ll just have to try again when life is a bit more stable. We all know how that usually turns out.

I cannot tell you how many times clients have told me that they are ‘forced’ to eat unhelpful food when they are hungry and there is nothing else around. Why? Because they have to eat. They believe it is better to eat something that is dragging them down than to not eat at all. While this is certainly true when you’re literally starving and in a survival situation, that pang you feel between lunch and dinner does not count as a survival situation (barring medical issues, of course). Learning to handle these times is crucial to staying on track because this is not only when most people fall off track completely, but also when the most extra money is spent. As you gain more control and get better at identifying the difference between craving and hunger, you'll know when the situation calls for control strategies and when the situation calls for simple satisfaction (a snack prepared for just these occasions).

Craving control strategies are vitally important. Waiting until the craving hits to try and come up with a plan is a guaranteed way to lose. If this book has tried to stress anything, it is that planning is the key to success. So how do you plan for the unplanned? The first step is to take the unplanned for granted. It's going to happen. But despite the millions of ways our plans can be interrupted, it's helpful to not overcomplicate the possibilities. As a rule, the unplanned event is going to be some situation that has you hungry and not able to access the food you prepared, either because you already ate it or you don't have it with you. In any case, a few steps of preparation can solve at least 80% of the possible problems.

Step 1. Identify whether the feeling is truly hunger or just a craving. When the gnawing ache in the pit of your stomach hits you, pull out a prepared snack and wash it down with a bottle of water. If the problem is actual hunger, this will take away the feeling within 7-15 minutes. If the problem is a craving, you will feel the same gnawing ache 15 minutes later despite the fact that you know your stomach has food in it. Once you have identified the feeling as a craving, the enemy of your flat stomach has just been unmasked. You are no longer fooled by the thought that you are depriving yourself of needed fuel. Now you know for a fact that your brain is just trying to fool you into eating the food it used to eat and you can resist it more effectively.

As an extra strategy, it is helpful to know where in your body the feeling is coming from. Hunger will almost always come from your stomach. If you feel like you want to eat something (maybe you passed an ad, had a memory triggered, are highly stressed, etc.) which you know is unhelpful, pay attention to whether you feel that craving in your stomach or in some other part of your body - head, chest, hands, etc. Most of the time, if you are feeling the 'hunger' emanating from your chest, it's just a craving and your body already has all it needs.

Step 2. Have a few small zip-loc bags of nonperishable, real-food snacks (mixed nuts are the easiest to prepare) stashed in places you would likely find yourself stuck and unprepared (vehicle, work desk, pockets). This way, if it is a genuine hunger problem, you will always have something close by that can help you stay focused until you are able to get a healthy meal again. Just remember to replenish the emergency snack if you have to use it.

Step 3. Always have water. Whether you decide to carry around a gallon jug or just have a few standard bottles handy, drinking water when you feel pangs of hunger can often help you get through to the next meal when there is nothing helpful around. There are two reasons for this. Firstly, the volume of water in your stomach will temporarily fool your body into thinking it has eaten and it will dampen the hunger response. Secondly, sometimes a feeling of hunger is actually our body signaling that it is dehydrated. Obviously, getting water into our system solves that problem.

Step 4. Utilize one of the following craving control strategies.

Chew sugar free gum. This will either relieve the craving or help distract you from it.

Give yourself permission to a treat...just not now. If you are craving tacos, tell yourself that you will eat as many tacos as you want on your designated treat meal. This does two things. 1) It keeps you from falling for your craving during a weak moment. 2) It keeps you from feeling deprived because you know that you will be eating the food you want within the week. It doesn't really feel like you're deprived when you've just given yourself permission to eat the treat you want. While you are not indulging at that very moment, you do know the exact moment when you will be indulging. That small compromise with your mind can often rid you of the craving entirely.

Fast Food Survival Tips

It's finally happened. You're caught without a prepared meal, you forgot to replenish the emergency snacks, the pangs of craving and/or hunger have hit, and all your attempts to calm them down have utterly failed and you can't concentrate on anything else but food. This is when nearly everyone falls off track. They give in and rush over to the nearest fast food place looking to just get something small on the dollar menu. But they already messed up so.....And that's how they get you. They coax people in with the option of a dollar menu, the realization hits that they have already fallen off the wagon by getting a burger so they might as well go all the way and upsize to a combo with fries and a drink. What started as a $1 "mini-cheat" turns into an $8 purchase and a nutritional train wreck that will often leave your body feeling gross. If you're caught in this predicament, what do you do? Here are a few survival tips that can keep the damage from an emergency drive-thru to a minimum.

1) Order water right away.

Instead of spending minutes perusing and letting the targeted marketing of the menu board conjure up more and more cravings, set the tone right away by ordering water. This sets the tone for the rest of your decision and keeps you from ordering one of the worst health offenders - soda.

2) Stick to first principles of healthy eating

You can have anything on the menu that you could technically harvest or kill. This precludes bread, breaded items (sorry, no onion rings or jalapeno poppers), sauces, and fries (nothing about that oil is natural). A lot of fast food restaurants offer some version of a salad. If their salad doesn't look at all appealing, you can order a burger or a chicken sandwich but, instead of taking them whole, ask for a to-go container with just the meat and vegetable portions of the sandwiches. They may look at you oddly but, let's be clear, your body is worth a lot more than an odd look or two. Also, you'll be spending a lot less money using these strategies than you would if you just grabbed a combo.

Good Rules vs Bad Rules

Rules That Make Things Harder (and their alternatives)

Bad Rule - “Drink 8 glasses of water a day.”

Problem - As we’ve said throughout this book, the more complicated you make the attempt, the more things you have to try to remember throughout the day, the harder it is going to be to stick to your plan. There are way too many responsibilities and distractions in our daily lives to pile on two dozen more to- dos to remember.

Real Rule - Drink enough water

Helpful Tip - Use a large water container (1/2 gallon or greater) which you will use throughout the day. Drink from it whenever you feel thirsty or get a chance. It’s with you which means there is no inconvenience attached to drinking. Furthermore, the fact that it’s in one container allows you to have one goal - finish one bottle of water by the end of the day. Simple. Easy. Convenient.

Bad Rule " -Eat six small meals a day to boost your metabolism."

Problem - If something is important enough, you can make it happen. However, finding the time to eat six small meals a day with all the demands we already have on our time is setting yourself up to fail. Our society is largely set up to allow for three meals a day and adding three more may be very difficult and could easily derail your progress.

While trying to eat six times a day could be worth it if the results were amazing, the reality is, unless you're training to be a competitive body builder, the difference in results between an appropriately portioned three-meal plan and six small meals a day is very minimal and not really worth the extra effort. Many of us trainers maintain a lean body fat percentage (10-12% for men, 18-20% for women) while eating three meals a day and experience no problems in doing so. Remember, don't stress about the best before you fix the basics.

Real Rule - Eat the appropriate number of calories with the appropriate nutrition.

Helpful Tip - The consistent average is much more

important to maintain than a perfect meal or perfect timing. Have a system that works with your life and keep it consistent.

Conclusion

Thus, it begins. You now have the critical mass of tools needed to begin forging he body, health, and lifestyle you want. When everyone else sees nothing, you can now look deeper and see the opportunities in the cracks and the scraps. You can see, take hold, and leverage all the 'nothing' to make real moves forward and upward.

The principles in this book apply too much more than nutrition. The goal is that you will use them to transform your body first. After you have done so, I hope your now-trained eyes and hands will be able to see and take action on the opportunities to grow and lead the life you really want - opportunities others either don't see or simply dismiss.

That is what this is all about. For too long, both ourselves and others have discounted us. We've been told, and we've believed, that the health, body, and life we truly want are for those with more money, more time, and more connections. We have been individually and systematically convinced of our powerlessness, our deprivation, and our brokenness. Powerful people and many large companies have used that mindset against us to con us out of a collective billions of dollars. What we didn't know, but that you know now, is that within that brokenness lies all the pieces we need to start out way up and out. We can use that scrappiness and apply it with honesty and strategy to accomplish what so many thought was out of reach. We may be broke right now. But we are done being broken. Here is the rest of your journey to a new body, new health, and a new life. Remember, right here, right now, you have what it takes.

Made in United States
Orlando, FL
02 November 2026

90104228R00076